NEW
JEWISH
COOKING

FOR HANNAH

NEW
JEWISH
COOKING

GROUNDBREAKING DAIRY-FREE KOSHER RECIPES
from BEVIS MARKS THE RESTAURANT

JASON PRANGNELL

Absolute Press

Publisher and Project Editor **Jon Croft** Commissioning Editor **Meg Avent** Editor **Jane Middleton**
Creative direction and design **Ian Middleton** at Design United Worldwide Photographer **Lisa Barber**
Props Stylist **Sue Rowlands** Food Stylist **Joy Skipper**

ISBN: 1904573444
ISBN 13: 9781904573449

First published in Great Britain in 2006 by Absolute Press, Scarborough House, 29 James Street West, Bath BA1 2BT
T: 44 (0) 1225 316013 F: 44 (0) 1225 445836 email: info@absolutepress.co.uk Website: www.absolutepress.co.uk

A CIP catalogue record of this book is available from the British Library
Printed and bound by Printer Trento, Italy

ACKNOWLEDGEMENTS

New Jewish Cooking would not have seen the light of day, if it had not been for Kenny & Susan Arfin's vision and drive
to bring kosher restaurants into the 21st century.

Their encouragement, passion and friendly nature, has made working at Bevis Marks a joy. Together we have grown and
blossomed to make The Restaurant what it is today, with one eye firmly focused on the future. Many thanks are also
afforded to all the staff who have helped and supported us along the way, without forgetting our families, friends and
most importantly our customers with whom the restaurant continues to flourish.

When our publisher Jon Croft and commissioning editor Meg Avent approached us, the opportunity was gratefully and
thankfully accepted to showcase what we were doing to a wider audience! Their enthusiasm, encouragement, wit and
know-how have made this book what it is.

Our gratitude is also extended to the team who helped produce this book. Ian Middleton for his vision and stunning
design, Lisa Barber for her acute and artistic photography, Joy Skipper for her support and styling, Jane Middleton for
editing the recipes with a keen eye and calming approach and also a special thanks to Matt Inwood at Absolute Press
must be passed on, along with praise for my darling Hannah for her endless hours of typing from my barely discernible
scribbles.

Thanks to David Steinhoff at the Sephardi Kashrut authority for all his support & guidence.

So much time and effort has gone into this book and I hope you enjoy reading and cooking from it as much as we have
all enjoyed producing it!

CONTENTS

BEVIS MARKS THE RESTAURANT

My grandmother came over to England from Russia in 1898 to escape the pogroms. She was one of eight children, five of them girls. All the sisters brought with them a combination of traditional Jewish and Eastern European recipes, and all of them were superb cooks.

After my grandfather died prematurely in 1946, my grandmother came to live with my family. I remember that throughout my childhood she would be standing at the stove from morning till night. She cooked superb traditional dishes, which was quite extraordinary because she could neither read nor write. I would often spend my time after school with her in the kitchen, watching and helping her cook. I think this is where my obsession with food began.

My family were kosher butchers, starting off with a shop in Petticoat Lane in London's East End, which was where most of the Jewish population had migrated to from Russia and Poland in the early 1900s. As a young boy during my school holidays I would help in the shop, learning about the best cuts of meat for different dishes and gaining a great deal of knowledge about kosher meat and poultry. After leaving school I went into my parents' kosher butcher business in north London and then later opened another branch in St John's Wood.

The kosher meat trade had always been very mundane and conservative – I desperately wanted to do something exciting and different. So I started producing my own chopped liver, potato latkes, stuffed breast of veal, rack of lamb, crown of lamb, stuffed peppers, boneless duck with apricot and minced chicken stuffing. Most of these things had never been seen before in kosher butcher's shopsand it revolutionised the business.

After the birth of our two children, Ross and Hayley, my wife Susan and I moved to Bournemouth to take over the only existing kosher butcher's there. I had always wanted to live on the coast and Bournemouth in those days was a leading holiday resort. Besides the 3,000 Jewish families that lived there, it attracted a lot of Jewish holidaymakers drawn to the many kosher hotels. One of the largest – and the only one that did outside catering – closed in the mid Eighties, which presented a great opportunity for someone to take over the catering side of the business.

Right: Kenny and
Susan Arfin at
Bevis Marks
The Restaurant

At last I saw a chance to pursue my ambition of bringing kosher food into the twentieth century. Susan and I catered for many successful weddings, barmitzvahs and parties. Guests would often ask us to come and cater for parties in London, and we became the nominated kosher caterers at many of London's five-star hotels, including the Hyde Park Hotel (now the Mandarin Oriental). In the end, we were so busy in London that we decided the time had come to move back there.

> This was the beginning of our journey to bring kosher food into the mainstream, somewhere Jewish people could be proud to bring non-Jewish friends and business associates.

The kosher restaurant scene in London was drab, boring and uninspiring. We felt that something had to be done. At the time, French-café-style dining was becoming immensely popular, with Café Rouge and similar chains opening up on every high street. Why couldn't there be a kosher version of this type of café? So, The Café on the Green was born in 1994 in Golders Green, a fashionable kosher dairy restaurant with cutting-edge food. For once, the Jewish public could eat the same standard of food and service that they would expect in any other restaurant or café, and in stylish surroundings. It was an instant success and was the focus of a lot of media interest. Café on the Green was featured on national television in 1998 in 'Taste of Britain' with Dorinda Hafner, a renowned Australian food critic and author. It became the prototype for many other modern kosher restaurants and there are now some 50 of them in northwest London.

At the time, the West End had only one kosher restaurant, which was actually a deli-diner. We felt there was a need for something more sophisticated to serve London's Jewish population of approximately 250,000, but it also had to appeal to the non-Jewish public. In November 2000 we opened a fine-dining kosher meat restaurant, Six-13. It was very well received by the Jewish community and won considerable press acclaim.

This was the beginning of our journey to bring kosher food into the mainstream, somewhere Jewish people could be proud to bring non-Jewish friends and business associates. After all, why should kosher food be enjoyed only by Jewish people? The whole concept behind it is that it is clean, healthy and good for you. Chicken soup, which is part of the staple diet, has even been proven to have antibacterial properties. All kosher meat cooking is completely non-dairy, as one of the main religious requirements forbids meat and milk products to be cooked or eaten together.

> We aim to provide
> affordable, fresh,
> delicious modern
> Jewish cuisine for City
> locals, business people
> and tourists alike.

While we were at Six-13 we were approached by one of the leading members of London's Sephardi community who wanted us to open a restaurant in the City. Finding a high-quality, reasonably priced meal in elegant surroundings in the City was notoriously difficult, and finding a kosher meal was totally impossible. Our first concern was to find a chef who was capable of cooking great food but without using any dairy produce – a hollandaise without butter and a brûlée without cream. He also had to be as passionate about food as we were. Jason Prangnell, our head chef, is just that person. His outstanding knowledge and energy can be found only among the country's top chefs – we had our perfect match!

In July 2003 we opened a meat restaurant in the heart of the City of London, at Bevis Marks, a Sephardi synagogue that also happens to be the oldest synagogue in Britain. Bevis Marks The Restaurant is situated in a beautiful hidden courtyard near Bishopsgate, in part of the synagogue's Grade I-listed 300-year-old building. It is the first kosher restaurant in the City for over ten years, since the closure of the iconic Blooms.

We aim to provide affordable, fresh, delicious modern Jewish cuisine for City locals, business people and tourists alike. While the dishes are fully kosher and completely suitable for the most observant Jewish person, the quality of the cuisine appeals across the board. We are excited to have the opportunity to showcase this in such unique surroundings. Bevis Marks The Restaurant marries the totally traditional with the totally modern.

Jason Prangnell's Modern British-influenced menu sets a new standard in kosher meat cooking. Traditional Jewish favourites such as the celebrated chicken soup with matzo balls and salt beef and chips feature alongside Modern British classics, including pâté de foie gras with apple and raisin chutney, and confit of duck with lavender mash, tomato confit and rosemary jus. The restaurant also serves Sephardi dishes with a twist, such as lamb and apricot tagine with couscous and beetroot harissa, and spiced salmon with haricot beans, piquillo peppers and coriander. Desserts include the much-loved lockshen (noodle) pudding, vanilla and peach crème brûlée, and pear and fig tarte tatin with prune and Cognac ice cream – all non-dairy.

We are thrilled that Bevis Marks The Restaurant has been recognised by Jewish and non-Jewish critics alike for its outstanding food, service and atmosphere, and we hope that you enjoy reading and cooking our recipes as much as we have enjoyed creating them.

Kenneth Arfin, August 2006

INNOVATIONS IN KOSHER CUISINE

Jason Prangnell, Head Chef, Bevis Marks The Restaurant

From the very start I realised that being Head Chef at Bevis Marks The Restaurant, was going to be something completely different and something very challenging!

Having spent the first decade of my cooking life in mainland Europe, dotted with many searching sojourns around the globe, discovering and getting to understand new cuisines and cultures, I had found myself once again back in Britain, where I spent five years in London before beginning my Bevis Marks journey in the late summer of 2003. Like most chefs of my generation in the UK I had been classically trained in the traditions of French and British cuisine. Having reached a certain standard and seniority I decided to move to central Europe to further my knowledge of food and life itself. There my horizons were expanded and I was encouraged, guided and taught, not just about the surrounding cuisines, but of the world's other great culinary treasures. I was fortunate to experience middle-eastern food, itself influenced by the Ottoman Turks, spicy Asian cooking with all its many different styles and flavours spanning from India to China, contrasting with the fresh and delicate approach of Japan. I was captivated by the robust and tropical offerings of south and central America, as well as with the foods of Africa and the Caribbean. Although unaware of it at the time these culinary adventures were to keep me in good stead for what lay ahead.

Most top restaurants' menus are based on prime cuts of meat, such as fillets, rumps, saddles and sirloin, along with seafood such as lobsters, prawns, scallops, mussels and the like, often accompanied, sauced and glazed with numerous dairy products. All of these ingredients suddenly became unattainable as I was now working in a 'kosher restaurant'! A quick crash-course in Jewish Dietary Laws, showed that all of these classical restaurant mainstays were forbibben.

So the not inconsiderable task lay ahead to create an innovative, modern menu that would entice and surprise its core audience. I also wanted to dispel the common belief that Jewish cooking was all stodge and dumplings. I wanted to open people's eyes to the many cuisines and cultures that Jewish communities around the world have taken in and then, out of dietary necessity, given their own distinctive imprint. Both for me as a chef and for my customers this break with tradition was like a breath of fresh air. I was forced to really think about how to get the best out of what foods I had available and to then draw on different styles and methods to bring out the very best of the produce available – a radically different approach when compared to the normal safe chefs' options of simply relying on expensive seafood and lavish cuts of meat. Well, I say expensive! This was my next shock! Although kosher is obtained from the traditionally cheaper cuts, the ethical and painstaking process needed to render it kosher makes it double or triple the price of non-kosher meat, thus making the chef's task of achieving a reasonable gross profit and help balance the books that much more difficult. This is the challenge that keeps me awake at night!

So the culinary challenge was set, along with physical restrictions of working in a tiny basement kitchen, affectionately called the 'The Shed', with myself and just one other chef. Now, three years on, we feel that we have achieved what we set out to do. We have received awards and praise from customers and critics alike. The pleasure is doubled in the knowledge that almost half of our customers aren't even Jewish, and some of them don't even realise they are in a kosher restaurant, thus mirroring the vision we originally set out with – to offer the Jewish kosher community something truly different, but something that everyone, from whatever community, could enjoy.

Lechayim!

Jason Prangnell August 2006

WHAT IS KOSHER? (THE LAWS OF KASHRUT)

The word kosher has long been used to denote anything that is genuine or legitimate, but its original and true meaning refers to the Jewish dietary laws laid down in the five books of Moses. These are interpreted, reviewed and set out by the Beth Din, the Rabbinical court that oversees all aspects of Jewish life and law.

Meat and dairy

The main observance is the strict separation of meat and dairy. Kosher restaurants must be either meat or dairy establishments. However, both can serve foods considered as pareve – i.e. ones that contain no meat or dairy products.

In the kosher home, the family will have different sets of crockery and cutlery and separate storage and refrigeration space to ensure total separation between meat and dairy meals, as would a large synagogue with two separate kitchens. At least three hours must elapse between the eating of meat and dairy meals.

Meat and fish

Meat and fish may not be cooked or eaten together, but you may eat one immediately after the other. It is customary, however, to cleanse the palate with a drink or a piece of bread in between.

Kosher meat

The rules governing kosher meat are another strict adherence. All kosher meat must be slaughtered in an ethical manner, in confinement (not in the presence of other animals) and by a highly trained slaughterer known as a shohet. The carcass is then checked for any blemishes or symptoms of disease, with the lungs, intestines and offal given special attention. This is followed by 'porging', which involves the removal of forbidden fats and veins. This process is very difficult in the hindquarter, particularly with larger animals, and outside Israel the hindquarter is generally sold on to the non-kosher trade (see the list of permitted cuts on page 16). Finally, for the meat to be given kosher status, it is salted and washed in water three times.

Liver

For liver to be kosher, it must be prepared in a special manner due to its blood content. It is scored, washed and salted, placed on a wire rack over a metal tray and roasted until no blood remains. It is then washed again, after which it is ready to use. The wire rack and tray used to catch the cooked blood must be kept and washed separately.

Kosher and forbidden animals

The basic rules for animals state that four-legged creatures must have cloven hooves and chew the cud – for example, cattle, goats, sheep and deer. Kosher venison is not normally available in the UK, however, as deer are shot in the open field, rendering them not kosher. Pigs are forbidden, as are birds of prey, ostriches and vultures. Kosher fowl include chicken, duck, goose and turkey. Though pigeon, partridge and pheasant are kosher, they must be caught or farmed in order to be slaughtered properly, and not shot, which would again render them not kosher.

Eggs

Before cooking, eggs must be checked by cracking them open and inspecting them for blood spots; eggs with these must be discarded. Fortunately, this does not apply to hardboiled eggs!

Fish

Only fish that have removable scales and fins are kosher. All other types of fish, including eels, sharks and shellfish, are not kosher (see the list of permitted fish on page 16).

Fruit and vegetables

All fruit and vegetables are kosher, but bugs and insects are strictly forbidden. This means that soft fruits, herbs, salads and leafy vegetables must be throughly checked and washed several times before use. Green asparagus is best avoided, as bugs can easily be trapped in its soft tips. It is also advisable to check all dried fruit, rice and beans.

Wine and grape juice

Wine and grape juice, grape-based spirits, liqueurs or drinks, along with wine and balsamic vinegars, must come from a rabbinical-approved source and carry a hechsher, or kosher seal. This is because many non-kosher wines and grape products are made or refined with non-kosher ingredients.

PERMITTED CUTS OF MEAT AND FISH

Terms in brackets denote particular kosher terminology.

MEAT

Beef

Kosher	Not kosher
Neck (chuck steak)	Hind shin
Fore shin (shin)	Sirloin
Flat ribs (top rib)	Fillet
Brisket	Rump
Chuck ribs	Silverside
Middle ribs	Topside
Fore ribs	
Prime bola	
Wing ribs	
Rib eye	
Thick flank	
Thin flank	

Veal

Kosher	Not kosher
Shoulder	Best end
Knuckle	Tendons
Neck	Loin
Low cutlets	Rump
(veal chops)	Cushion
Breast	Under cushion
	Shin
	Thick flank

Lamb

Kosher	Not kosher
Scrag end	Best-end saddle
Shoulder	Chump
Middle neck	Leg
Best-end neck	
Breast	

FISH

Common fish species

Kosher	Not kosher
Anchovy	Catfish
Bass	Caviar
Bream	Cockles
Brill	Crab
Carp	Crayfish
Cod	Dogfish
Grey mullet	Eel
Gurnard	Huss
Haddock	Langoustine
Halibut	Lobster
Herring	Monkfish
Mackerel	Mussels
Plaice	Prawns
Red mullet	Ray
Red snapper	Rock salmon
Salmon	Scallops
Sardines	Shark
Sole	Skate
Trout	Sturgeon
Tuna	Swordfish
	Turbot
	Whelks

JEWISH FESTIVALS

The Jewish calendar is based on the 13 lunar cycles of the year, beginning with Tisheri, which falls in September or October.

Tisheri
Cheshvan
Kislev
Teves
Shevat
Adar 1
Adar 2
Nisan
Iyar
Sivan
Tamuz
Av
Elul

Rosh Hashanah (The Jewish New Year)
1st and 2nd Tisheri (September/October)
Rosh Hashanah commences at sunset and is celebrated for two days. Pomegranates, 'the fruit of Israel', are eaten, as are figs, dates, raisins and quince. Apples are cut up and dipped in honey, in the hope of a sweet and prosperous coming year.

Yom Kippur (The Day of Atonement)
10th Tisheri (September/October)
Yom Kippur is a day of fasting and prayer – a time of reflection, remembrance and charity. The meal before the fast is plain and simple. The fast is broken with a cold drink of almond milk or apricot or cherry juice, followed by a dairy meal and sweet pastries. Later in the day it is customary to cleanse the palate with water and a piece of bread before the second meal. This meal contains chicken to honour the custom of 'Atonement', where a chicken is koshered for every member of the family.

Sukkot (The Feast of Booths/Harvest Festival)
15th Tisheri (September/October)
During this eight-day festival, Jews must spend their time under a sukkah – a booth or hut built with plants and branches to represent the temporary shelters used during the time in the wilderness between Egypt and the Promised Land.

In the restaurant our retractable glass roof panels are opened and decorated with leaves, branches and many seasonal fruits, which traditionally include figs, grapes, dates, oranges, pomegranates, lemons and the symbolic plants of palm, myrtle and willow.

Simchat Torah (The Rejoicing of Law)
23rd Tisheri (September/October)
This marks the end of Sukkot, with the reading of the first and last portions of the five books of Moses.

Hanukkah (The Festival of Lights)
25th Kislev (December)

Hanukkah celebrates the miracle of the cruse of olive oil, which burned for eight days in the holy temple after it had been sacked and desecrated by the Syrian Hellenists in 165BC. Today a nine-branched candlestick is lit, one for each night of the eight-day festival, with the central ninth candle used to light the others.

The festival of lights is celebrated with many foods deep-fried in oil, such as potato latkes, doughnuts and meat and vegetable fritters, along with curds, soured cream and cheesecakes.

Purim (The Festival of Lots)
14th Adar (February/March)

Purim commemorates the story of Queen Esther, who outwitted the Persian Haman 2,000 years ago, after he decreed a death sentence for all Jews. The festival now also recognises all the times that Jews have escaped persecution. It is the only festival where heavy drinking is encouraged as a way of celebration and joy.

The main meal can be either vegetarian or fish and dairy. Pastries with plums and many foods containing poppy seeds are eaten as a symbolic gesture.

Pesach (Passover)
15th Nisan (March/April)

This festival celebrates the exodus of Jews from Egypt and the birth of Judea. During this time no leavened bread or grains, or beans that can ferment, can be eaten or stored in a kosher home or premises. These products can be sold to non-Jews and then bought back after the festival has ended. Just before Passover begins, the ritual spring-clean and search for wayward crumbs, known as 'the search for hametz', must be completed. Then the special Passover crockery and cutlery are brought out and matzo (unleavened bread) is allowed inside the house.

The Sedar table is the sacred meal at the beginning of Passover. It is adorned with matzos, along with five symbolic foods:
A green vegetable dipped in salt (karpas)
A bitter herb (maror)
A roasted egg (betza)
A lamb shank bone (zeroa)
A fruit and nut paste (haroset)

Shavuot (Pentecost)
6th Sivan (May/June)

Pentecost celebrates the Jews receiving the Torah – the book that contains the Ten Commandments – on Mount Sinai, and their birth as a holy nation. This is a festival of dairy foods to honour the land of milk and honey, and to respect the fact that there was no time to kosher meat after leaving Mount Sinai.

ASHKENAZI AND SEPHARDI COOKING

Jewish culture and cuisine can be broadly divided into two strands: Ashkenazi and Sephardi.

Ashkenazi Jews are mainly of central and eastern European origin and are also found in large numbers in the USA. Their food is the cold-weather cooking of northern countries, with hearty dishes such as knishes, kugels, latkes and tzimmes. Flavourings are subtle but there is a fondness for sweet and sour sauces, particularly with fish and meat.

Sephardi Jews originate from the Iberian peninsula and include North African, Asian and Middle Eastern settlers. Their cooking reflects the bold spicing of these areas, and makes abundant use of herbs, olive oil, garlic and lemon. Typical dishes include tagines, dolmades, pilaus and kebabs.

NOTE FOR AMERICAN READERS

In the recipes, American measures are given in brackets after the metric measures. Below are the American terms for some of the ingredients and equipment used in this book.

aubergine = eggplant
baking parchment = wax paper
baking sheet = cookie sheet
beetroot = beets
broad bean = fava bean
caster sugar = superfine sugar
celeriac = celery root
chips = French fries
chick peas = garbanzo beans
cider = apple cider
cider vinegar = apple cider vinegar
cling film = plastic wrap
coriander = cilantro (when referring to
  the green, leafy herb rather than the seeds)
cornflour = cornstarch
courgette = zucchini
dried yeast = active dry yeast
flaked almonds = slivered almonds
frying pan = skillet
grey mullet = mullet, striped bass
grill = broiler
grilled = broiled
groundnut oil = peanut oil
gurnard = searobin
hard-boiled egg = hard-cooked egg
haricot beans = navy beans
hazelnut = filbert

icing sugar = confectioner's sugar
kitchen paper = paper towels
lamb's lettuce = corn salad, mâche
Little Gem lettuce = use small Romaine lettuce
loaf tin = loaf pan
mackerel = Atlantic mackerel
minced beef = ground beef
palette knife = metal spatula
pastry cutter = cookie cutter
pepper, red, green or yellow = bell pepper,
  red, green or yellow
pine nut = pignola
plain flour = all-purpose flour
porcini mushrooms = cèpes
red bream = porgy
roasting tin = roasting pan
rocket = arugula
salt beef = corned beef
sieve = strainer
spring onion = scallion
strong white flour = bread flour
swede = rutabaga
sweetcorn = corn kernels
tomato purée = tomato paste
Tomor margarine = kosher margarine
vanilla pod = vanilla bean

STOCKS & SOUPS

CHICKEN BROTH

We use this flavoursome stock as the basis for numerous soups, sauces and meat dishes. It is particularly good in a light-bodied red wine gravy and, of course, the Jewish mainstay, chicken soup (see page 26).

Place the chicken wings in a roasting tray, drizzle with the vegetable oil and roast in an oven preheated to 200°C/400°F/Gas Mark 6 until they are light golden. Drain off the oil and put the wings in a large saucepan. Add the chicken thighs, the whole vegetables, the bay leaves, thyme, peppercorns and salt and cover with the water. Bring to the boil, skim off any scum from the surface, then reduce the heat and simmer for 5–6 hours, until you have a golden broth. Pass through a fine sieve, leave to cool, then refrigerate.

Once chilled, remove excess fat from the top of the broth. It will keep, covered, in the fridge 2–3 days, or it can be frozen for up to 1 month.

MAKES ABOUT 2 LITRES
(8 CUPS)

1kg (2¼ pounds) chicken wings
2 tablespoons vegetable oil
2 chicken thighs
1 large onion, peeled
2 carrots, peeled
3 celery sticks
2 bay leaves
1 sprig of thyme
10 black peppercorns
1 tablespoon sea salt
2.5 litres (10 cups) water

FISH STOCK

MAKES ABOUT 1.25 LITRES (5 CUPS)

1 tablespoon vegetable oil

1 onion, finely sliced

1 celery stick, finely sliced

1 leek (white part only), finely sliced

4 shallots, finely sliced

2 garlic cloves, finely sliced

1kg (2¼ pounds) raw fish bones

125ml (½ cup) dry white wine

1.25 litres (5 cups) water

zest of 1 lemon

2 sprigs of dill

Use this stock for poaching fish and for making fish sauces, soups and accompaniments to fish dishes. The best bones to use are from white flat fish, such as sole, plaice and halibut. Try to avoid bones from oily fish, as they can produce a slightly bitter stock.

Heat the olive oil in a large saucepan, add the vegetables and garlic and cook gently for 2–3 minutes without colouring. Then add the fish bones and wine, increase the heat and cook for 5 minutes. Pour in the water and bring to the boil, skimming any scum from the surface. Then add the lemon zest and dill and simmer for 20 minutes. Pass the stock through a fine sieve and leave to cool. It will keep, covered in the fridge for a day, or it can be frozen for up to 1 month.

VEGETABLE STOCK

MAKES ABOUT 1.5 LITRES (6 CUPS)

2 large onions

5 carrots

6 celery sticks

2 leeks (white part only)

3 garlic cloves, peeled but left whole

2 bay leaves

2 sprigs of thyme

4 parsley stalks

10 black peppercorns

250ml (1 cup) dry white wine

1.25 litres (5 cups) water

This stock is good for adding flavour to vegetable and vegetarian dishes. It is also useful for letting down strong or over-reduced meat and fish sauces, soups and casseroles.

Roughly chop all the vegetables into 2cm (¾-inch) pieces. Place in a large saucepan with all the rest of the ingredients and bring to the boil. Simmer for half an hour, then strain through a fine sieve and leave to cool. The stock will keep for 2–3 days in the fridge or a month in the freezer.

CHICKEN SOUP WITH MATZO BALLS

Chicken soup is known as Jewish penicillin and is every grandmother's cure for a cold. Perhaps it owes its reputation to its high levels of vitamin B6, zinc and iron. It's certainly tasty enough to pick up anyone who is feeling under the weather. The dumplings for this speciality are made with matzo meal, which is ground from the unleavened matzo bread that is served at Passover.

First make the matzo balls. Whisk the egg, duck fat or margarine and chicken broth together, then mix in the matzo meal, ground almonds and some salt and pepper. Cover with cling film and chill for 30 minutes (this allows the mixture to absorb the liquid and firm up). Then roll the mix into walnut-sized balls between the palms of your hands; it should make at least 8. Place the dumplings in a pan of boiling salted water and simmer for 20 minutes, until cooked and slightly puffed up.

Cook the pasta in plenty of boiling salted water until tender, then drain. Bring the chicken broth to the boil and divide between 4 soup bowls. Add the pasta, matzo balls, carrot cubes, seasoning and chives.

SERVES 4

100g (4 ounces) taglierini pasta

1 litre (4 cups) Chicken Broth (see page 24)

1 carrot, cooked and cut into 5mm (1/4-inch) cubes

1/2 teaspoon sea salt

1/4 teaspoon ground white pepper

1 tablespoon snipped chives

FOR THE MATZO BALLS:

1 large egg

1 tablespoon duck fat or Tomor margarine, melted

3 tablespoons warm Chicken Broth (see page 24)

75g (2/3 cup) matzo meal

1 tablespoon ground almonds

sea salt and black pepper

CHILLED CAULIFLOWER AND FENNEL SOUP

This fragrant, cooling soup is an ideal way to begin a summer lunch. The subtle aniseed flavour of the fennel complements the mildness of the cauliflower. You could garnish it with thin strips of smoked salmon, which also works well with cauliflower.

Gently fry the onion in the olive oil for 5–6 minutes without colouring. Add the fennel and cauliflower and cook for 5 minutes. Then add the hot vegetable stock and bay leaf, bring to the boil and simmer for 30 minutes, until the vegetables are very soft. Remove the bay leaf and blitz the soup with a hand blender until smooth.

Season to taste with salt and pepper. Allow to cool, then chill thoroughly, preferably overnight. Serve in soup plates, drizzled with lemon oil and garnished with the chopped dill.

SERVES 4–6

1 onion, cut into 2cm (^{3}/$_4$-inch) dice

4 tablespoons olive oil

2 fennel bulbs, finely sliced

1 large cauliflower, cored and finely chopped

1 litre (4 cups) hot Vegetable Stock (see page 25)

1 bay leaf

lemon oil, for drizzling

1 tablespoon chopped dill

sea salt and ground white pepper

BUTTERNUT SQUASH SOUP

SERVES 6

1kg (2¼ pounds) butternut squash, peeled, deseeded and cut into 2cm (¾-inch) dice

100ml (scant ½ cup) olive oil

1 tablespoon cumin seeds

1 tablespoon coriander seeds

2 large onions, cut into 2cm (¾-inch) dice

1 litre (4 cups) hot Vegetable Stock (see page 25)

1 tablespoon lime juice

4 teaspoons pumpkinseed oil

2 tablespoons pumpkin seeds

sea salt and black pepper

This autumn and winter vegetable makes a very healthy soup, high in beta-carotene and low in calories. The seeds of the squash can be cleaned, lightly roasted and used as a garnish for this soup, or just served as a tasty snack.

In a large saucepan over a high heat fry the diced squash in the olive oil until golden brown. Add the cumin and coriander seeds and fry for a minute. Reduce the heat, add the onions and sweat for 4–5 minutes, until softened. Then pour in the hot vegetable stock, bring to the boil and simmer for 30 minutes or until the squash is very soft. Remove from the heat and blitz with a hand blender until smooth.

Pour the soup through a fine sieve. Season to taste with sea salt, pepper and the lime juice. Serve in soup bowls, drizzled with the pumpkin seed oil and sprinkled with the pumpkin seeds.

GAZPACHO WITH HERB CROSTINI

Here we have a couple of Mediterranean combinations: the famous chilled Spanish soup with the warm Italian toast, and the classic combination of tomato and oregano. The word gazpacho comes from the Spanish and Portuguese caspos, denoting a piece of leftover bread. A gazpacho should contain bread, oil and vinegar. It can be hot or cold, white, green, or the more familiar red, tomato-based soup.

Add the tomatoes to a large pot of boiling water, in batches, leave for 10–15 seconds, then remove with a slotted spoon and immediately refresh in a bowl of iced water. Peel off the skins, cut the tomatoes in half and scoop out and discard the seeds.

In a food processor, blitz together the onion, yellow pepper, cucumber and garlic until they form a rough purée. Add the tomato flesh and breadcrumbs and blitz in short bursts to retain the rough texture until the tomato and bread are fully combined. Finally stir in the chilli oil, vinegar, tomato juice and chilled water and season to taste with sea salt and freshly ground black pepper. Chill for 2–3 hours.

For the crostini, lay the ciabatta slices on a baking tray, drizzle with the olive oil and sprinkle with the oregano. Season with salt and pepper and bake in an oven preheated to 220°C/425°F/Gas Mark 7 for 5–6 minutes, until crisp and golden brown. Serve the soup with the crostini on the side.

SERVES 4

1kg (2¼ pounds) ripe plum tomatoes

1 red onion, chopped

1 yellow pepper, deseeded and chopped

1 cucumber, deseeded and chopped

2 garlic cloves, finely sliced

100g (2 cups) fresh breadcrumbs

3 tablespoons chilli oil

3 tablespoons white wine vinegar

250ml (1 cup) tomato juice

250ml (1 cup) chilled water

sea salt and black pepper

FOR THE CROSTINI:

½ ciabatta loaf, finely sliced

100ml (scant ½ cup) olive oil

2 tablespoons chopped oregano

PUY LENTIL AND BORLOTTI BEAN SOUP WITH PESTO

We always offer a vegetarian soup at the restaurant and this is one of our favourites. This version of pesto, of course, contains no cheese, making it vegan as well as kosher.

Heat the olive oil in a large saucepan, add the onions, carrots and celery and fry gently for 5 minutes without colouring. Increase the heat and add the ground spices and tomato purée. Fry for 1 minute, then add the lentils, tomatoes and hot vegetable stock. Bring to the boil, add the bay leaves and simmer for 45 minutes or until the lentils are tender. Add the borlotti beans and simmer for 5–10 minutes. Season to taste with salt and pepper and serve in warm soup bowls, drizzled with the pesto.

SERVES 4

3 tablespoons olive oil

2 red onions, cut into 5mm (¼-inch) dice

2 carrots, cut into 5mm (¼-inch) dice

3 celery sticks, finely sliced

1 teaspoon ground cumin

1 teaspoon smoked paprika

1 tablespoon tomato purée

100g (⅔ cup) Puy lentils

200g (scant 1 cup) canned chopped tomatoes

750ml (3 cups) hot Vegetable Stock (see page 25)

2 bay leaves

200g (1 cup) canned borlotti beans, drained

4 tablespoons Pesto (see page 174)

sea salt and black pepper

SPLIT PEA SOUP WITH PARSLEY

SERVES 4–6

2 tablespoons groundnut oil

50g (2 ounces) smoked beef, finely diced

1 onion, finely diced

1 carrot, finely diced

2 celery sticks, finely sliced

1 tablespoon dried mint

1 tablespoon Worcestershire sauce

200g (1 cup) dried split peas, soaked overnight in plenty of cold water, then drained

1 litre (4 cups) hot Chicken Broth (see page 24)

1 bay leaf

2 tablespoons chopped parsley

sea salt and black pepper

200g (1 cup) canned borlotti beans, drained

4 tablespoons Pesto (see page 174)

sea salt and black pepper

An English classic dating from the time of Charles Dickens, when London was often covered in dense smog. This soup acquired the name, London Particular, from the nickname for the smoky fog (a 'pea souper'). In the restaurant we use a kosher Worcestershire sauce made without anchovies, complying with the kosher law of not combining meat and fish.

Heat the groundnut oil in a large saucepan, add the smoked beef, onion, carrot and celery and fry over a medium heat for 5 minutes without colouring. Then add the dried mint and Worcestershire sauce and cook for 2 minutes. Stir in the split peas, followed by the hot broth and bay leaf. Bring to the boil and simmer for 45 minutes. Remove the bay leaf and purée the soup with a hand blender until smooth. Pass through a fine sieve, reheat and season to taste. Serve in warm soup bowls, sprinkled with the chopped parsley.

TOMATO AND BULGAR SOUP
WITH FRESH MINT AND LEMON

This hearty soup makes a wonderful winter warmer. Scented with smoked paprika, it is a take on the classic Turkish wedding soup, ezo gelin, made with red lentils and cracked wheat. Although chicken broth gives this soup a bit of extra body, a vegetarian version made with vegetable stock can be just as good.

Heat the olive oil in a saucepan, add the onion and fry gently for 5 minutes without colouring. Add the smoked paprika, ground coriander and tomato purée and fry for 2 minutes. Mix in the bulgar, then pour in the hot broth. Stir well, bring to the boil and simmer for 20–25 minutes, until the bulgar is soft. Season to taste with salt and pepper and stir in the mint. Serve immediately, with the lemon wedges at the side, preferably accompanied by some warm bread.

SERVES 4

3 tablespoons olive oil

1 large onion, finely diced

1 teaspoon smoked paprika

1 teaspoon ground coriander

3 tablespoons tomato purée

175g (1 cup) bulgar (fine cracked wheat)

1 litre (4 cups) hot Chicken Broth (see page 24)

2 tablespoons chopped mint

1 lemon, cut into 8 wedges

sea salt and black pepper

BROAD BEAN SOUP WITH RICE AND DILL

Broad beans, also known as fava beans, are a favourite throughout the Sephardi world, used in soups, stews and salads. They can also form the basis of the Middle Eastern finger food, falafel.

These are made with dried broad beans or chickpeas, which are cooked, finely ground, then moulded into balls and deep fried. You could replace the rice and dill garnish for this soup with a drizzle of garlic oil and a sprinkling of toasted flaked almonds, two other flavours that marry very well with the beans.

Heat the oil in a saucepan, add the onion and garlic and fry gently for 5 minutes without colouring. Increase the heat to high, stir in the ground spices and fry for another minute. Add the hot chicken broth and the broad beans and boil for 15 minutes. Then add the diced potatoes, return to the boil and simmer for 45 minutes. Blitz to a smooth purée with a hand blender, then pass through a fine sieve. Return the soup to the pan, bring back to the boil and season to taste. Serve in warmed soup bowls, garnished with the dill and rice.

SERVES 4–6

3 tablespoons olive oil

1 onion, cut into 1cm (1/2-inch) dice

2 garlic cloves, finely sliced

1 tablespoon ground cumin

1 tablespoon ground fennel seeds

1 litre (4 cups) hot Chicken Broth (see page 24)

250g (1 1/4 cups) dried broad beans, soaked overnight in cold water, then drained

350g potatoes, peeled and cut into 1cm (1/2-inch) dice

1 tablespoon chopped dill

4 tablespoons cooked rice

sea salt and ground white pepper

ISRAELI BEEF AND VEGETABLE SOUP

SERVES 4

2 tablespoons olive oil

300g (11 ounces) beef chuck steak, cut into 1cm (½-inch) dice

2 onions, cut into 1cm (½-inch) dice

2 carrots, cut into 1cm (½-inch) dice

3 celery sticks, cut into 1cm (½-inch) dice

2 garlic cloves, finely diced

1 tablespoon ground cumin

1 teaspoon ground turmeric

1 teaspoon ground fenugreek

1 green chilli, halved, deseeded and finely sliced

750ml (3 cups) hot Chicken Broth (see page 24)

1 large potato, peeled and cut into 1cm (½-inch) dice

2 tablespoons coriander leaves

2 tablespoons finely chopped parsley

sea salt and black pepper

This aromatic and hearty broth is traditionally served during the Jewish New Year (Rosh Hashanah) to promote good health and luck for the coming year. It can also be served with various chilli- or herb-based sauces or pastes stirred into the broth. My version is a delicate combination of all the traditional flavours, without being too overpowering.

Heat the olive oil in a large saucepan, add the beef and fry over a high heat until nicely browned. Add the onions, carrots and celery and fry for 2 minutes. Stir in the garlic, ground spices and chilli and fry for another minute. Pour in the hot broth, bring to the boil and simmer for 40 minutes. Add the diced potato, bring back to the boil and simmer for 20 minutes. Season to taste with salt and pepper and serve in warmed soup plates, sprinkled with the herbs.

STARTERS

CRISPY THAI SALT BEEF WITH CORIANDER

This dish was born of a need to use the tailpiece of a whole side of cooked salt beef brisket, which tends to crumble when sliced across the grain. It was inspired by an ancient Thai salad of deep-fried salt beef garnished with deep-fried garlic and shallots. These could also be used to give the dish a bit of extra crunch. The quantities below have been given for just one person because it's important to cook this dish in small quantities, otherwise the beef will stew instead of fry. You can, of course, prepare it for more than one but you will need to cook each portion separately.

Cut the spring onion into long, thin strips and leave in a bowl of iced water for 10–15 minutes so they curl up. Drain and pat dry. Heat the groundnut oil in a wok, add the salt beef and stir-fry for 2–3 minutes, until crisp. Add the bean sprouts and stir-fry for another minute. Then add the sweet chilli sauce and cook for 1–2 minutes, until slightly caramelised. Fold in the coriander leaves and then serve, using tongs to pile everything up in the centre of the plate. Garnish with the spring onion and coriander sprigs.

SERVES 1

1 spring onion

2 tablespoons groundnut oil

75g (3 ounces) cooked salt beef, shredded

100g (4 ounces) bean sprouts

1 tablespoon Thai sweet chilli sauce

2 tablespoons coriander leaves

2 sprigs of coriander, to garnish

PÂTÉ DE FOIE GRAS WITH APPLE AND RAISIN CHUTNEY

SERVES 10–12

375ml (1½ cups) red wine

1 onion, finely diced

2 garlic cloves, peeled

2 sprigs of thyme

200g (7 ounces) chicken livers, koshered (see page 44)

400g (14 ounces) kosher foie gras

2 large eggs

375g (13 ounces) Tomor margarine, melted

150ml (²/₃ cup) soya cream

50ml (3 tablespoons) brandy

sea salt and ground white pepper

Apple and Raisin Chutney (see page 175) and Orange and Pomegranate Sauce (see page 170), to serve

a handful of salad leaves, dressed with Honey and Mustard Dressing (see page 166), to garnish

Pâté de foie gras is rumoured to originate from the Jewish community of Alsace in eastern France. The production of fattened goose liver dates back to Roman times, when the geese were force fed with figs. In modern times maize is used to achieve an enlarged liver, which usually weighs 600–900g (1¼–2 pounds). We source our koshered foie gras from Strasbourg, where the livers are pink and firm compared to the softer, ivory-coloured livers from Toulouse in southwest France.

Put the red wine, onion, garlic and thyme in a saucepan and bring to the boil. Simmer until the liquid has almost completely evaporated. Remove the thyme and place the onion mixture in a food processor with the chicken livers. Blitz to a smooth purée, then add the foie gras and eggs and blitz again until smooth. Pass the mixture through a fine sieve into a large measuring jug or bowl, then add the melted margarine, soya cream, brandy and some salt and pepper. Blitz with a hand blender until completely emulsified.

Line a 1-litre (4-cup) terrine mould with 2 layers of cling film and pour in the mixture. Cover the top of the terrine with cling film, then with the lid. Place in a deep roasting tray half filled with cold water and bake in an oven preheated to 160°C/325°F/Gas Mark 3 for 45 minutes. Leave to cool and then refrigerate overnight.

To serve, turn the terrine out of the mould on to a board and carefully remove the cling film. Mop up any liquid with kitchen towel and cut the terrine into slices. Serve each slice with a tablespoon of chutney, a drizzle of the sauce and a handful of dressed salad leaves. Accompany with warm toast.

THYME-CURED SALMON WITH CHAMP POTATO SALAD

A lovely springtime dish with a Celtic twang – from the traditional champ combination of potato and spring onions to the fish that is gently flavoured in the spirit of the Highlands. You need to prepare the salmon at least 2 days in advance. If you can obtain some wild salmon for this dish, do use it. It is in season from March to August and its firmer texture and superior flavour mean that it lends itself very well to curing and smoking.

Put the salmon in a baking dish, skin-side down. Mix together the salt, sugar, dried thyme, juniper and lime juice and zest and spread this mixture over the top of the salmon. Cover with cling film and refrigerate for 24 hours. Wash off the salt mix with cold water and pat the fish dry. Skin the salmon and place it back in the dish. Pour over the whisky, then mix the fresh thyme and mustard together and spread them over the top of the salmon. Cover with cling film and leave to marinate for 1–2 days.

To make the salad, cook the potatoes in boiling salted water until tender, then drain. Cut into quarters when cool enough to handle. Combine with the mayonnaise and spring onions and season to taste.

Put the salmon on a board and cut it into very thin slices on the diagonal. To serve, place a spoonful of potato salad on each plate and drape over 4–5 overlapping slices of salmon. Garnish with a sprig of thyme.

SERVES 6–8

400–500g (14–18-ounce) piece of salmon fillet, skin on

150g (5 ounces) fine sea salt

50g (¼ cup) dark brown sugar

1 tablespoon dried thyme

1 tablespoon juniper berries, crushed

juice and grated zest of 2 limes

50ml (3 tablespoons) malt whisky

2 tablespoons fresh thyme leaves, plus a few sprigs of thyme to garnish

2 tablespoons coarsegrain mustard

FOR THE CHAMP POTATO SALAD:

750g (1 pound 10 ounces) new potatoes, scrubbed

3 tablespoons mayonnaise

8 spring onions finely sliced

sea salt and black pepper

CHOPPED LIVER WITH SPICED FIG COMPOTE

Along with chicken soup, what could be more Jewish than chopped liver? For liver to be kosher, it must be salted and seared on a grill or in a hot oven to remove its blood, rendering it almost cooked, so it requires minimal cooking. Figs are mentioned many times in the Bible, eaten fresh or dried, and make a wonderful compote to complement chopped liver. Serve with rye bread or warm toast.

Heat the duck fat or groundnut oil in a large frying pan, add the onions and fry gently for 5–6 minutes, until softened but not coloured. Add the livers and warm through for about 2 minutes. Place the onions and liver in a food processor with the boiled eggs and brandy and blitz to a rough purée. Season to taste with salt and pepper.

Leave to cool, then chill for 2–3 hours. Serve with the spiced fig compote and warm toast.

SERVES 4

2 tablespoons duck fat or groundnut oil

250g (9 ounces) onions, cut into 1cm (1/2-inch) dice

250g (9 ounces) chicken livers, koshered (see page 44)

2 large eggs, hard boiled

25ml (2 tablespoons) brandy

sea salt and black pepper

4 tablespoons of Spiced Fig Compote (see page 175), to serve

MATJES HERRING WITH APPLE AND RED ONION

SERVES 4

1 red onion, peeled, quartered and finely sliced

1 Granny Smith apple, cored, quartered and finely sliced

2 tablespoons mayonnaise

4 double fillets of cured herrings (matjes)

100g (4 ounces) mixed salad leaves

2 tablespoons Honey and Mustard Dressing (see page 166)

sea salt and black pepper

A Dutch and German speciality, matjes herrings are large fillets preserved in brine, resulting in a wonderfully mild flavour. When served with a traditional sauce of apple and onion bound with mayonnaise, this dish is generally referred to as 'housewife's style', because the recipe is traditionally passed down from generation to generation.

To make the sauce, combine the red onion, apple and mayonnaise and season to taste. Divide between 4 plates and lay 2 herring fillets on each plate. Toss the salad leaves with the dressing, season with salt and pepper and use to garnish the plates.

CHICKEN AND BULGAR SALAD WITH FIG, ORANGE AND WILD ROCKET

This is a beautiful warm salad with different tastes, textures and vibrant colours, using produce from all around the Mediterranean.

Peel the oranges, removing all the white pith, and cut out all the segments from between the membranes, holding them over a bowl to catch the juice. Squeeze the membrane to extract the remaining juice and set aside.

Put the bulgar in a bowl and pour the chicken broth over. Mix well, cover with cling film and leave for 10 minutes, then fluff up with a fork.

Season the chicken cubes. Heat 1 tablespoon of the olive oil in a frying pan, add the chicken and sauté until golden brown and fully cooked. Pull the pan off the heat, add the balsamic vinegar and orange juice and stir to scrape up all the juices from the base of the pan. Stir in the rest of the olive oil to make the salad dressing.

Mix the wild rocket, bulgar, chicken and dressing together in a bowl and season to taste. Divide between 4 plates and garnish with the fresh figs and orange segments.

SERVES 4

2 oranges

50g ($\frac{1}{4}$ cup) bulgar (fine cracked wheat)

100ml (scant $\frac{1}{2}$ cup) boiling Chicken Broth (see page 24)

2 chicken breasts, skinned and cut into 1cm ($\frac{1}{2}$-inch) cubes

3 tablespoons olive oil

1 tablespoon balsamic vinegar

100g (4 ounces) wild rocket

4 fresh figs, each cut into 6

sea salt and black pepper

SEARED TANDOORI TUNA WITH CUCUMBER AND RADISH SALAD

The tandoori-style combination of tamarind and ginger complements oily fish very well, with its slightly sweet acidity. We occasionally do grilled tandoori-marinated mackerel instead, served with a purple potato salad. Interestingly, there used to be a Jewish community in and around Bombay and Calcutta dating back hundreds of years, but in recent decades it has almost disappeared.

To make the marinade, mix together the tamarind, ginger, tomato purée and ground spices. Coat the tuna with half the marinade and refrigerate for 30 minutes. Wipe off the marinade and pat the tuna dry, then season with salt. Heat the olive oil in a non-stick frying pan until very hot, add the tuna and sear for 30 seconds on each side. Remove from the pan and coat with the rest of the marinade. Place in the freezer for 30 minutes.

For the salad, mix together the cucumber, radishes, coriander, 1 teaspoon of the lime juice and the groundnut oil. Season to taste with salt and pepper. For the dressing, mix the mayonnaise with 1 tablespoon of water and the remaining lime juice and season with salt.

To serve, place the salad in the middle of 4 plates and drizzle with the dressing. Cut the seared tuna into slices 1cm (½-inch) thick and place on top of the salad. Sprinkle with coarse sea salt and the poppy seeds.

SERVES 4

2 tablespoons tamarind paste

2 tablespoons ginger purée

1 tablespoon tomato purée

1 teaspoon ground cumin

1 teaspoon ground fennel seeds

1 teaspoon smoked paprika

2 pieces of fresh tuna, each about 8 x 4 x 4cm (3 x 1½ x1½ inches)

1 tablespoon olive oil

1 teaspoon poppy seeds

sea salt and black pepper

FOR THE CUCUMBER AND RADISH SALAD:

½ cucumber, halved lengthways, deseeded and finely sliced

8 red radishes, halved and finely sliced

4 tablespoons coriander leaves

2 teaspoons lime juice

2 tablespoons groundnut oil

2 tablespoons mayonnaise

BEEF HOLISHKES WITH SWEET AND SOUR TOMATO SAUCE

Holishkes are a meat-filled vegetable dish served during Sukkot (harvest festival). This is a more refined version but still champions the humble cabbage.

SERVES 4

75g (scant ½ cup) basmati rice

1 large Savoy cabbage

2 tablespoons duck fat or olive oil

1 onion, finely chopped

1 tablespoon crushed garlic

400g (14 ounces) minced beef

1 tablespoon chopped parsley

1 tablespoon matzo meal

1 egg yolk

1 teaspoon smoked paprika

500ml (2 cups) hot Chicken Broth (see page 24)

sea salt and black pepper

FOR THE SWEET AND SOUR TOMATO SAUCE:

1 tablespoon olive oil

125g (½ cup) tomato purée

75g (scant ½ cup) dark brown sugar

2 tablespoons cider vinegar

Put the rice in a small pan with 150ml (²/₃ cup) water and a pinch of salt and bring to the boil. Cover and simmer for 10 minutes, until the water has evaporated and the rice is tender. Spread the rice over a small tray and leave to cool. Cut out the core from the base of the cabbage and separate the leaves, being careful not to tear them. Cut out the tough stem from the outer leaves with a small sharp knife. Blanch the cabbage leaves in boiling water for 2 minutes, until softened, then drain and refresh in iced water immediately. Carefully squeeze out excess water and pat dry with a towel.

Heat the duck fat or olive oil in a pan, add the onion and garlic and fry gently for 4–5 minutes, until softened but not coloured. Place in a mixing bowl and add the minced beef, cooked rice, parsley, matzo meal, egg yolk, smoked paprika and some salt and pepper. Mix well, then divide the mixture into 12 pieces and roll each one into a small cylinder. Wrap each one in the cabbage leaves. You will need 1–2 leaves per roll, depending on the size; the filling should be completely enclosed. Place in a small, deep roasting tin. Carefully pour the hot stock over the parcels and tightly cover the tray with foil. Place in an oven preheated to 180°C/350°F/Gas Mark 4 and bake for 25–30 minutes, until the stuffing is firm and cooked through. Drain, reserving the cooking liquor, and keep warm.

To make the sauce, heat the olive oil in a small pan, add the tomato purée and fry over a medium heat for 2 minutes. Add the sugar and vinegar and cook for a minute, stirring all the time. Add 300ml (1¼ cups) of the reserved cooking liquor, bring to the boil and simmer for 5 minutes. Season to taste. To serve, pour the sauce into the centre of 4 plates and place 3 holishkes on each one.

CARROT AND APRICOT KOFTES WITH LAMB'S LETTUCE, HERB AND GARLIC SAUCE

SERVES 4

500g (1 pound 2 ounces) carrots, peeled and cut into 5mm (¼-inch) dice

6 tablespoons fresh breadcrumbs

2 tablespoons pine nuts

3 tablespoons finely diced dried apricots

1 tablespoon matzo meal

1 teaspoon ground coriander

½ teaspoon smoked paprika

4 spring onions, finely sliced

2 tablespoons finely chopped parsley

2 tablespoons finely chopped mint

2 tablespoons finely chopped dill

1 large egg, beaten

plain flour, for dusting

100ml (scant ½ cup) olive oil

100g (4 ounces) lamb's lettuce

sea salt and black pepper

FOR THE SAUCE:

3 tablespoons mayonnaise

1 tablespoon water

1 tablespoon lemon juice

½ teaspoon crushed garlic

1 tablespoon finely chopped dill

1 tablespoon finely chopped parsley

These vegetarian koftes are a Turkish staple. They are very popular in Istanbul, where there is a Judeo-Spanish community that combines traditional Sephardi cuisine with local Turkish specialities and also classic French dishes.

Put the carrots in a saucepan, add enough water to cover and a pinch of salt and boil for 15 minutes, until soft. Drain well, then return to the pan over a low heat. Mash and stir the carrots with a wooden spoon for 1–2 minutes to help them dry out a little, then remove from the heat. Add the breadcrumbs, pine nuts, apricots, matzo, spices, spring onions, herbs, egg and some seasoning and mix to form a smooth, soft paste. Transfer to a bowl and chill for 30 minutes.

On a floured work surface, divide the mixture into 12 and, with lightly floured hands, roll each one into a small oval shape. Dust with flour and set aside. Heat the oil in a large non-stick frying pan, add the koftes and fry over a medium heat for about 2 minutes on each side, until golden brown.

For the sauce, simply whisk all the ingredients together in a bowl.

To serve, put 3 koftes on each plate with a handful of lamb's lettuce and a spoonful of the sauce by its side.

BEETROOT SALAD WITH SALT BEEF AND HORSERADISH ICE CREAM

This dish came about because of our fascination with Heston Blumenthal's savoury ice creams at the Fat Duck restaurant in Bray. So we wanted a kosher equivalent! The obvious solution was to use salt beef, with the traditional matching relish of beetroot and horseradish (chrane). The combination works well either hot or cold, so why not frozen? After a little experimentation, this dish was born, and won praise from customers and critics alike.

For the ice cream, place the salt beef, horseradish and soya milk in a saucepan and bring to the boil, then remove from the heat. Whisk the egg yolks and sugar together, then gradually add the hot milk mixture and whisk well. Return the custard to a clean saucepan and cook over a low heat, stirring constantly, until the custard thickens enough to coat the back of the spoon. Remove from the heat, add the soya cream and mix well. Pour into a bowl and leave to cool, then chill thoroughly. Churn in an ice-cream machine and freeze for 5–6 hours or overnight.

For the salad, mix the cucumber, shallot, vinegar and oil together and season with salt and pepper. To serve, cut each beetroot into 6 slices and fan them out in a semi-circle on 4 serving plates. Place a scoop of ice cream in the middle with a spoonful of the cucumber mixture, then garnish with a sprig of dill or chervil.

SERVES 4

3 tablespoons finely diced cucumber

1 tablespoon finely diced shallot

1 teaspoon cider vinegar

1 tablespoon groundnut oil

4 cooked beetroot, peeled

sea salt and black pepper

sprigs of dill or chervil, to garnish

FOR THE SALT BEEF AND HORSERADISH ICE CREAM:

3 tablespoons finely chopped cooked salt beef

1 tablespoon freshly grated horseradish

250ml (1 cup) soya milk

5 egg yolks

75g ($\frac{1}{3}$ cup) caster sugar

250ml (1 cup) unsweetened soya cream

WARM CHICKEN LIVERS WITH WATERCRESS AND DANDELION SALAD AND PICKLED WALNUTS

This is a good old traditional English dish, with peppery watercress from the southern counties coupled with sharp young walnuts, which are soaked in brine, then pickled with malt vinegar and various spices. Their acidity marries well with the mild chicken livers, creating a lovely balance of flavours.

Dandelion salad is a long, thin, white-stemmed salad vegetable with small, pointy yellow or green leaves. It can be found at some farmers' markets and specialist greengrocer's shops. It also grows wild across northern Europe and is popular in France, where it is known as pissenlit.

Check the livers, removing any sinew, and break them into bite-sized pieces. Heat the oil in a frying pan until very hot, then add the livers and sauté for 2 minutes to heat through. Remove from the heat and set aside.

For the salad, tear the dandelions into 5cm (2-inch) pieces and place in a bowl. Add the watercress and dressing and toss well.

To serve, divide the salad between 4 plates and lightly scatter the warm chicken livers and pickled walnuts over it.

SERVES 4

400g (14 ounces) chicken livers, koshered (see page 44)

1 tablespoon groundnut oil

100g (4 ounces) dandelion salad

1 bunch of watercress, tough stalks removed

2 tablespoons Honey and Mustard Dressing (see page 166)

4 pickled walnuts, roughly chopped

SMOKED DRIED TURKEY WITH WHITE ASPARAGUS

SERVES 4

500g (1 pound 2 ounces) white asparagus, peeled

juice and grated zest of 1 lemon

1 shallot, finely chopped

1 bay leaf

1 teaspoon sea salt

2 tablespoons Honey and Mustard Dressing (see page 166)

1 tablespoon snipped chives

12 slices of smoked dry-cured turkey

Although it is now available all year round, from all over the world, asparagus is best during its natural season of late spring/early summer. This is when the thin green spears traditionally grown in the Vale of Evesham, running from Stratford-on-Avon to Warwickshire, are available, together with white spears from Europe. There is also a wild variety known as Bath asparagus, or the wood star of Bethlehem. Those who keep kosher are encouraged to stick to white asparagus. White Asparagus is often served in Europe, hot with grilled meats and fish or cold with smoked fish or cured meats.

Remove the tough base of the asparagus stalks (about 3–4cm/1½ inches), then cut the stalks in half on the diagonal. In a large saucepan, bring 1 litre (4 cups) of water to the boil with the lemon juice, zest, shallot, bay leaf and salt. Add the asparagus and cook for 4–5 minutes, until just tender. Remove with a slotted spoon and pat dry.

Mix the dressing with the chives and 1 tablespoon of the asparagus cooking liquor. Remove the bay leaf and strain the remaining cooking liquor through a fine sieve to catch the shallots. Add these to the dressing.

To serve, divide the asparagus between 4 plates, drizzle with the dressing and put the slices of smoked turkey on top.

FISH

ROAST GURNARD WITH JERUSALEM ARTICHOKES, SORREL AND MUSTARD SAUCE

This is a wonderfully robust warm starter, using the much underrated and very good-value red gurnard. Also somewhat neglected is the Jerusalem artichoke. Originating from America, it is similar to a knobbly potato, with a taste faintly reminiscent of globe artichokes. In fact it is part of the sunflower family, and the Italian name for sunflower, girasole, sounds similar to Jerusalem, hinting at the origin of its name.

In a large saucepan, bring 1 litre (4 cups) of water to the boil with the lemon juice and 1 teaspoon of sea salt. Add the Jerusalem artichokes and boil for 10–15 minutes, until cooked but still a little firm to the touch. Meanwhile, heat the olive oil in a large frying pan until very hot, add the gurnard fillets, skin-side down, and cook for 3–4 minutes, pressing down on the fillets to stop them curling up. Season with salt and pepper and turn the fillets over. Reduce the heat and cook for 2–3 minutes more, then set aside.

Warm the mustard sauce together with the sorrel in a small saucepan. Drain the Jerusalem artichokes and divide between 4 plates. Pour the sauce around and place the fish on top.

SERVES 4

juice of ½ lemon

500g (1 pound 2 ounces) Jerusalem artichokes, scrubbed and cut into slices 1cm (½-inch) thick

2 tablespoons olive oil

4 x 100g (4-ounce) red gurnard fillets

250ml (1 cup) Coarsegrain Mustard Sauce (see page 163)

2 tablespoons finely sliced sorrel leaves

sea salt and black pepper

BAKED HALIBUT WITH MUHAMMAR RICE AND COFFEE SAUCE

SERVES 4

4 tablespoons olive oil

4 cardamom pods

1g (a large pinch) saffron strands

300g (1½ cups) basmati rice

600ml (2½ cups) hot fish stock (see page 25)

1 tablespoon rosewater

2 tablespoons honey

4 x 175g (6-ounce) halibut fillets

1 quantity of Red Wine Fish Sauce (see page 166)

1 teaspoon instant coffee

8 sprigs of coriander

sea salt and ground white pepper

This dish is influenced by the pearl divers of the Middle East, with whom muhammar rice is very much associated. Traditionally it was served with their daily catch of fish. Here we have the majestic halibut with a mild, sophisticated coffee sauce, which combines perfectly with the subtly sweet cardamom-scented rice.

Heat half the olive oil in a saucepan, add the cardamom pods and fry over a medium heat for 1 minute. Add the saffron, stir in the rice and fry for a further minute. Then add the hot fish stock, rosewater and honey, bring to the boil and simmer for 10 minutes, stirring occasionally.

Remove from the heat, season to taste and cover with a lid. Meanwhile, brush the halibut fillets with the remaining olive oil, season with salt and pepper and place on a baking sheet lined with baking parchment. Bake in an oven preheated to 220°C/425°F/Gas Mark 7 for 7–8 minutes, until soft and opaque. Meanwhile, reheat the sauce, if necessary, and dissolve the coffee in it.

To serve, spoon the rice into the centre of each plate and top with the fish. Pour the sauce around and garnish with the sprigs of coriander.

SPICED MACKEREL WITH DATE AND MINT COUSCOUS AND HARISSA BROTH

This dish is inspired by the Moroccan Sephardi practice of stuffing oily fish with dates and rice and serving them with harissa and couscous. This refined version uses mackerel fillets and is moistened by a spicy broth. You could also garnish it with toasted flaked almonds, which work well with both fish and dates.

For the couscous, heat the olive oil in a saucepan, add the shallots and fry over a low heat for 2 minutes without colouring. Add the couscous and stir well. Pour in the hot vegetable stock and cook for 5 minutes, stirring occasionally. Remove from the heat, add the dates and mint and mix well. Cover with a lid and set aside.

For the mackerel, combine the olive oil with the ground spices in a large bowl, add the fish fillets and coat well. Season with salt and pepper and cook under a hot grill, skin-side up, for 5–6 minutes, until the skin is slightly crisp and the flesh is just done. Meanwhile, whisk the harissa into the hot stock and season to taste.

Serve the couscous in shallow bowls, topped with the mackerel and surrounded by the broth.

SERVES 4

4 tablespoons olive oil

1 teaspoon ground ginger

1 teaspoon ground cinnamon

1 teaspoon ground turmeric

½ teaspoon smoked paprika

8 x 75g (3-ounce) mackerel fillets

1 teaspoon harissa paste

400ml (1⅔ cups) hot Fish Stock (see page 25)

sea salt and black pepper

FOR THE DATE AND MINT COUSCOUS:

2 tablespoons olive oil

2 shallots, finely sliced

200g (1¼ cups) couscous

200ml (scant 1 cup) hot Vegetable Stock (see page 25)

75g (½ cup) dates, finely chopped

2 tablespoons finely chopped mint

RED BREAM WITH ROAST BEETROOT AND BABY RED CHARD

Although bream is thought of as a Mediterranean fish, red and black bream are also found in British waters. This is a light and colourful dish, perfect for a late-summer lunch or supper.

Put the beetroot and potatoes on a roasting tray lined with baking parchment and mix with 1 tablespoon of the olive oil. Season with salt and pepper, then roast in an oven preheated to 220°C/425°F/Gas Mark 7 for 20–25 minutes.

Brush the fish fillets with the remaining olive oil and season with salt and pepper. Lay them on top of the vegetables, skin-side up, and bake for 7–8 minutes, so the skin is slightly brown and the flesh is just done.

To serve, place the beetroot and potato in the middle of each plate and add a small handful of chard leaves. Drizzle liberally with the lemon dressing, place the fish on top and sprinkle with the chopped dill.

SERVES 4

2 beetroot, peeled and cut into 1cm ($^1/_2$-inch) wedges

300g (11 ounces) new potatoes, cut in half

2 tablespoons olive oil

4 x 150g (5-ounce) red bream fillets

100g (4 ounces) baby red chard leaves

150ml ($^2/_3$ cup) Lemon Dressing (see page 167)

2 tablespoons chopped dill

sea salt and black pepper

SEA BASS WITH AUBERGINE CAVIAR, BRAISED LEEKS AND RED WINE SAUCE

This is a lovely, deep-coloured, soft-textured dish with, of course, no caviar, as the sturgeon fish from which caviar is obtained is not kosher. Instead the term caviar refers to the aubergine's small, seed-like texture when roasted. It marries perfectly with sea bass, as they are both Mediterranean mainstays.

First prepare the aubergine caviar. Cut the aubergines in half lengthways and score the flesh in a criss-cross pattern with a small, sharp knife. Season with salt and pepper, brush each half with a tablespoon of olive oil and ½ teaspoon of garlic, then sandwich the aubergines back together and wrap tightly in foil. Bake in an oven preheated to 200°C/400°F/Gas Mark 6 for 40 minutes, until very soft. Unwrap the aubergines, scoop out all the flesh and chop finely. Heat the remaining olive oil in a frying pan, add the pine nuts and fry until lightly browned. Add the aubergine, tomatoes and parsley and cook for 2 minutes. Season to taste and keep warm.

To cook the bass, place the fillets, skin-side up, on a baking tray lined with baking parchment, season with salt and pepper and brush with 1 tablespoon of the olive oil. Bake in an oven preheated to 200°C/400°F/Gas Mark 6 for 7–8 minutes, until the skin is slightly browned and the flesh just done. Meanwhile, gently cook the leeks in the remaining olive oil over a medium heat for 5–6 minutes, until softened. Season to taste.

To serve, spoon the aubergine caviar into the centre of each plate, top with the leeks and then with the bass. Spoon the sauce around.

SERVES 4

4 x 175g (6-ounce) sea bass fillets

2 tablespoons olive oil

400g (14 ounces) trimmed leeks, finely sliced

200ml (scant 1 cup) Red Wine Fish Sauce (see page 166)

sea salt and black pepper

FOR THE AUBERGINE CAVIAR:

2 large aubergines

5 tablespoons olive oil

2 tablespoons crushed garlic

2 tablespoons pine nuts

1 tablespoon finely chopped sun-blushed tomatoes

2 tablespoons chopped parsley

BLACK BREAM WITH FENNEL, SUN-BLUSHED TOMATOES AND OREGANO

SERVES 4

2 fennel bulbs

6 tablespoons olive oil

4 x 175g (6-ounce) black bream fillets

4 tablespoons sun-blushed tomatoes, drained

2 tablespoons chopped oregano

100ml (scant ½ cup) Lemon Dressing (see page 167)

sea salt and black pepper

Here we have two classic combinations: fish with fennel and tomato with oregano. The mild aniseed flavour of fennel complements the sweet flesh of the bream, while any Italian will tell you that tomato and oregano is a marriage made in heaven. Sun-blushed tomatoes are semi-dried and marinated in herbs and olive oil, producing a lovely sweet flavour. With their vivid colour and subtle acidity, they really give this dish a lift.

Cut each fennel bulb into 8 wedges, place on a baking tray and drizzle with 4 tablespoons of the olive oil. Season with salt and pepper and roast in an oven preheated to 200°C/400°F/Gas Mark 6 for 15 minutes. Brush the bream fillets with the remaining olive oil and season with salt and pepper. Lay the fillets over the fennel and return to the oven for 7–8 minutes, until the fish is just done.

To serve, scatter the tomatoes and oregano over each plate and add the roasted fennel. Drizzle with the dressing and place the bream on top.

SEA BASS WITH WATERCRESS, ARTICHOKES AND CITRUS JUICE

Baked fish can sometimes be masked by powerful citrus fruits such as lemon and lime but orange and grapefruit are less acidic. They combine well with peppery watercress, which is one of the few salad leaves indigenous to southern Britain, grown in chalk aquifers in Hampshire, Dorset and Wiltshire.

With a sharp knife, peel the grapefruit and orange, removing all the white pith. Then, over a bowl to catch the juice, cut out the segments from between the membranes. Squeeze the membranes to extract the remaining juice. Cut the segments in half and set aside.

Place the sea bass fillets on a baking tray lined with baking parchment. Brush with the olive oil and season with salt and pepper. Bake in an oven preheated to 200°C/400°F/Gas Mark 6 for 7–8 minutes, until the skin is slightly browned and the flesh is just done.

To serve, place the artichokes in the centre of each serving plate and top with the watercress. Spoon the citrus segments and juice around the plate and finally put the sea bass on top of the salad.

SERVES 4

1 pink grapefruit

1 large orange

4 x 150g (5-ounce) sea bass fillets

2 tablespoons olive oil

300g (11 ounces) marinated artichokes, well drained

100g (4 ounces) watercress, tough stalks removed

sea salt and black pepper

GREY MULLET WITH SWISS CHARD AND CIDER SAUCE

SERVES 4

2 tablespoons groundnut oil

4 x 175g (6-ounce) grey mullet fillets

1 red onion, finely sliced

600g (1 pound 5 ounces) Swiss chard, finely shredded

300ml (1¼ cups) Cider Sauce (see page 163)

sea salt and black pepper

A firm and tasty coastal fish, grey mullet goes well with any sort of greens and a flavoursome sauce. Instead of Swiss chard, you could use the oriental bok choy with soy and chilli sauce, scattered with coriander.

Heat the oil in a large, non-stick frying pan, add the grey mullet fillets, skin-side down, and fry over a high heat for 3–4 minutes, until crisp and brown. Season with salt and pepper, turn the fillets over and cook for about 3–4 minutes, until just done. Quickly remove the fish and keep warm. Add the red onion and Swiss chard to the pan and stir-fry for 2–3 minutes, until wilted. Season to taste. In a small pan, gently reheat the cider sauce.

To serve, place the stir-fried greens in the centre of each plate, put the fish on top and pour the sauce around.

SPICED SALMON WITH HARICOT BEANS, PIQUILLO PEPPERS AND CORIANDER

This is a quick and hearty dish combining ideas from both sides of the Mediterranean. You could use any type of fish or beans. Bottled piquillo peppers have a lovely flavour but marinated red or yellow peppers would work just as well. Serve with new potatoes or Saffron Rice (see page 112).

Heat 1 tablespoon of the olive oil in a saucepan, add the red onion and garlic and fry gently for 5–6 minutes, until soft. Increase the heat, add the tomato purée and fry for 2 minutes, then add the chopped tomatoes, haricot beans and piquillo peppers. Cook for 10–15 minutes, stirring occasionally.

Meanwhile, mix the spices and lime zest with a tablespoon of the remaining olive oil and rub this mixture over the salmon fillets. Heat the remaining olive oil in a non-stick frying pan, place the salmon in it skin-side down and cook over a high heat for 3–4 minutes, until the skin is browned and crisp. Reduce the heat and turn the salmon over to finish cooking (about another 4–5 minutes). Season with salt, pepper and the lime juice.

To serve, stir the coriander leaves into the haricot bean mixture, divide between 4 plates and top with the salmon.

SERVES 4

3 tablespoons olive oil

1 red onion, cut into 1cm (½-inch) dice

2 garlic cloves, finely chopped

1 tablespoon tomato purée

400g (1⅔ cups) canned chopped tomatoes

250g (1¼ cups) canned haricot beans, drained

200g (7 ounces) piquillo peppers, cut into 1cm (½-inch) dice

1 tablespoon hot smoked paprika

1 tablespoon ground coriander

1 teaspoon ground turmeric

1 teaspoon fennel seeds

juice and grated zest of 1 lime

4 x 175g (6-ounce) pieces of salmon fillet

4 tablespoons coriander leaves

sea salt and black pepper

SEARED TUNA WITH TABOULEH AND CHICKPEA SALAD

Tabouleh is a popular salad in Sephardi areas and all over the Middle East, although it is particularly associated with Lebanese cuisine. It is traditionally served with Cos lettuce leaves, which are used to scoop up the salad. Here it is served with tuna, which is marinated and spiced with smoked paprika to give a barbecue flavour. It's ideal for a lazy summer lunch.

Mix 2 tablespoons of the olive oil with the smoked paprika and rub it over the tuna steaks. Set aside to marinate. Meanwhile, make the tabouleh. Put the bulgar or couscous in a bowl and pour over the boiling fish stock. Cover with cling film and leave for 10 minutes, then fluff up with a fork. Mix in the herbs, spring onions, tomatoes and chickpeas, stir in 50ml (3 tablespoons) of the dressing and season to taste.

Heat the remaining olive oil in a non-stick frying pan, add the marinated tuna steaks and sear over a very high heat for 1 minute on each side, until lightly browned on the outside but still rare inside. Season to taste with salt and pepper.

To serve, divide the tabouleh between 4 plates and place the tuna steaks on top. Drizzle with the rest of the lemon dressing.

SERVES 4

3 tablespoons olive oil

1 tablespoon smoked paprika

4 x 150g (5-ounce) tuna steaks

FOR THE TABOULEH AND CHICKPEA SALAD:

6 tablespoons bulgar (fine cracked wheat) or couscous

150ml ($^2/_3$ cup) boiling fish stock (see page 25)

1 bunch of flat-leaf parsley, finely chopped

2 tablespoons finely chopped mint

4 spring onions, finely sliced

2 plum tomatoes, deseeded and diced

200g (1 cup) canned chickpeas, drained

200ml (scant 1 cup) Lemon Dressing (see page 167)

TROUT WITH SAUERKRAUT, BRATKARTOFFELN AND PAPRIKA SAUCE

SERVES 4

4 tablespoons groundnut oil

2 onions, finely chopped

6 juniper berries, crushed

1 bay leaf

400g (14 ounces) sauerkraut

300ml (1¼ cups) Riesling wine

300ml (1¼ cups) Fish Stock (see page 25)

8 x 75g (3-ounce) trout fillets

750g (1 pound 10 ounces) new potatoes, boiled, peeled and sliced

1 teaspoon smoked paprika

200ml (scant 1 cup) Paprika Sauce (see page 168)

sea salt and black pepper

Pickled cabbage in the form of sauerkraut is a central European delicacy, full of vitamin C and healthy enzymes. It is widely available in jars and cans. Serving it with bratkartoffeln (fried potatoes) and a Paprika Sauce gives it a specifically German feel. An even more authentic touch would be to use zander, a common Central European freshwater fish, similar to trout.

Heat half the groundnut oil in a large saucepan, add half the onions and fry over a high heat until lightly browned. Add the juniper berries, bay leaf and sauerkraut and cook for 2–3 minutes, stirring all the time. Add the wine and allow to reduce for 2 minutes, then season with salt and pepper. Pour in the fish stock, reduce the heat and cook for about 20 minutes, until most of the liquid has evaporated.

Lay the trout fillets over the sauerkraut and place a lid on the pan, so the fish is braised with the sauerkraut; this will take about 4–5 minutes. Meanwhile, heat the remaining oil in a large frying pan, add the sliced potatoes and sauté until nicely browned. Add the remaining chopped onion and the smoked paprika and fry for a further 2 minutes, until the onion is lightly browned.

To serve, place the potato in the centre of each plate, top with the sauerkraut and criss-cross 2 trout fillets over. Gently heat the paprika sauce and spoon it around the edge.

SMOKED HADDOCK WITH NEW POTATOES, GREEN BEANS AND MUSTARD SAUCE

This is classic comfort food and so easy to prepare, with the main ingredients just added to a steamer at different stages to ensure even cooking. You could use either an electric steamer or a bamboo steamer over a saucepan of boiling water – either way, you will have a fragrant and healthy dish.

Cut each fish fillet in half and season with black pepper. Place the sliced potatoes in a steamer and steam for 2–3 minutes. Add the haddock pieces and steam for 5 minutes. Finally add the green beans and steam for 2 minutes more. Meanwhile, gently warm the sauce in a small saucepan.

To serve, place the potatoes in the centre of each plate, top with the beans and then with the haddock. Spoon the sauce around.

SERVES 2

2 x 150g (5-ounce) pieces of smoked haddock fillet

300g (11 ounces) new potatoes, cut into slices 1cm (1/2 inch) thick

150g (5 ounces) green beans, topped and tailed

150ml (2/3 cup) Coarsegrain Mustard Sauce (see page 163)

black pepper

MEAT

GRILLED RIB-EYE STEAK WITH HOME-MADE CHIPS, TOMATOES AND BÉARNAISE SAUCE

Steak and chips, the bistro classic, is universally loved, served with special sauces and a variety of garnishes. Here it is combined with moist grilled tomato, a sharp béarnaise sauce and peppery watercress, all of which complement grilled or roast beef beautifully.

Brush the rib-eye steaks and tomato halves with the olive oil, season with salt and pepper and set aside.

For the béarnaise sauce, put the vinegar, shallot, tarragon stalks and white peppercorns in a small saucepan, bring to the boil and simmer until reduced by half. Strain the vinegar reduction into a small bowl and discard the solids. Add the egg yolks to the vinegar and whisk well, then return to the pan. Whisk over a low heat until the mixture begins to thicken. Remove from the heat and very slowly add the melted Tomor, whisking all the time, so the sauce emulsifies and thickens. Finally add the chopped tarragon and chervil, season to taste and set aside.

Cook the steaks and tomatoes to your liking on a hot grill pan. Garnish with the watercress and serve with the béarnaise sauce and chips.

SERVES 4

- 4 x 200g (7-ounce) rib-eye steaks
- 2 plum tomatoes, cut in half
- 2 tablespoons olive oil
- 1 bunch of watercress, tough stalks removed
- Home-made Chips (see page 110)
- sea salt and black pepper

FOR THE BÉARNAISE SAUCE:

- 125ml (½ cup) white wine vinegar
- 1 shallot, finely sliced
- 4 sprigs of tarragon, leaves chopped (keep the stalks)
- 8 white peppercorns, crushed
- 3 egg yolks
- 250g (1 cup) Tomor margarine, melted
- 1 tablespoon chopped chervil

BRAISED BEEFSTEAK WITH GARLIC MUSHROOMS AND SPÄTZLE

Spätzle is a kind of fresh egg pasta, popular in central Europe, especially in Austria, southern Germany and Switzerland. Traditionally served with stews and braised dishes, it is also very good on its own, garnished with fried onions, cheese and fresh herbs.

Season the steaks with salt and pepper. Heat 2 tablespoons of the olive oil in a deep, non-stick frying pan, add the steaks and cook over a high heat for 2 minutes on each side, until lightly browned. Then add the sliced onion and fry for a minute longer. Add the white wine and simmer until reduced by half. Pour in the chicken broth, bring to the boil and simmer for 7–8 minutes.

Meanwhile, mix the mushrooms with the remaining olive oil and the garlic and season to taste. Place on a small baking tray and bake in an oven preheated to 220°C/425°F/Gas Mark 7 for 10 minutes, until tender.

Serve the steaks with the sauce spooned over and accompanied by the mushrooms and warmed spätzle, sprinkling everything with the chopped parsley.

SERVES 4

4 x 200g (7-ounce) rib-eye steaks

6 tablespoons olive oil

1 red onion, finely sliced

150ml (2/3 cup) dry white wine

300ml (1 1/4 cups) hot Chicken Broth (see page 24)

4 large Portobello mushrooms, cut into quarters

2 garlic cloves, crushed

1 quantity of Spätzle (see page 120)

2 tablespoons chopped parsley

sea salt and black pepper

TRADITIONAL SALT BEEF WITH HOME-MADE CHIPS AND CHRANE

SERVES 4

1.25kg (2¾ pounds) salted beef brisket

2 onions, peeled and halved

4 carrots, peeled and topped and tailed

6 celery sticks, trimmed

½ bunch of thyme

3 bay leaves

6 parsley stalks

12 black peppercorns

100ml (scant ½ cup) cider vinegar

4 sprigs of flat-leaf parsley, to garnish

Home-made Chips (see page 110) and Chrane (see page 172), to serve

Salt or corned beef has been a speciality of the Jewish kitchen for over 50 years, served in New York delis and London's East End bagel shops. Recently it has moved into restaurants, served with latkes or chips and accompanied by New Green Cucumbers (see page 172), another Jewish speciality.

Place the beef, vegetables, herbs, peppercorns and vinegar in a large saucepan and add enough water just to cover. Bring to the boil, cover with a lid and simmer for 2½ hours or until the meat is tender. Remove the brisket and rest on a chopping board for 4–5 minutes, then slice thinly across the grain. Garnish with the parsley sprigs and serve with the chips and chrane.

VEAL CHOPS MILANESE WITH HERB POLENTA AND TRUFFLE OIL

A classic north Italian combination of breaded veal and soft polenta, with a posh tomato sauce (very Milan). Fashion conscious or not, this dish really hits the spot.

First make the polenta. Heat the olive oil in a medium saucepan, add the shallots and garlic and fry over a low heat for 2–3 minutes without colouring. Add the polenta and fry for another minute, then add the chicken broth and mix well. Cook, uncovered, over a low heat for 40–45 minutes, stirring occasionally, until all the liquid has been absorbed and the polenta is soft. Mix in the chopped herbs, season to taste and keep warm.

Season the veal chops with salt and pepper. Coat them in the flour, then in the eggs, and finally in the breadcrumbs. Heat the olive oil in a large frying pan, add the chops and fry until golden brown on both sides. Transfer to a baking sheet lined with baking parchment and bake in an oven preheated to 190°C/375°F/Gas Mark 5 for 8–10 minutes.

Serve the chops on the polenta, drizzled with truffle oil, with the Milanese sauce spooned to the side.

SERVES 4

4 x 200g (7-ounce) veal chops

150g (1 cup) plain flour

3 eggs, whisked with 1 tablespoon water

150g (3 cups) breadcrumbs

4 tablespoons olive oil

white truffle oil for drizzling

300ml (1¼ cups) Milanese Sauce (see page 162)

sea salt and black pepper

FOR THE HERB POLENTA:

1 tablespoon olive oil

2 shallots, finely diced

1 teaspoon crushed garlic

150g (1¼ cups) fine polenta (not the instant variety)

750ml (3 cups) hot Chicken Broth (see page 24)

1 tablespoon chopped parsley

1 tablespoon chopped oregano

LAMB AND CHERRY KORESH WITH JEWELLED RICE

A koresh is a Persian stew, with many exotic spices and flavourings combining to create a wonderfully aromatic dish. Jewelled rice is another Persian classic. It is cooked in many stages and layers, eventually being formed into a pyramid shape with a crusty bottom layer of rice. This version, however, is a quick and moist pilaf, with the traditional ingredients showcased to accompany the homely koresh.

Heat the olive oil in a large saucepan, add the diced lamb and fry over a high heat for 7–8 minutes, until nicely browned on all sides. Add the onions and ground spices, mix well and fry for 2 minutes. Then add the chicken broth, rosewater, lime juice and zest, honey and cherries and bring to the boil. Reduce the heat, cover and simmer gently for 2 hours, until the meat is tender.

For the jewelled rice, heat the olive oil in a saucepan, add the shallots and orange zest and fry gently without colouring for 2 minutes. Add the rice, stir well and cook for a further minute. Then add the raisins, apricots and vegetable stock. Bring to the boil and simmer for 10 minutes, stirring occasionally, until all the liquid has been absorbed.

Meanwhile, for the carrots, bring the water, sugar and orange juice to the boil in a separate pan, add the carrot strips and simmer for 10 minutes, until slightly translucent. Drain well, discarding the liquid, and add to the rice, along with the almonds and pistachios. Serve the koresh in warmed shallow bowls, accompanied by the jewelled rice.

SERVES 4

4 tablespoons olive oil

800g (1³/₄ pounds) boned lamb shoulder, cut into 3cm (1¹/₄-inch) dice

2 large onions, cut into 2cm (³/₄-inch) dice

1 teaspoon ground coriander

1 teaspoon ground turmeric

1 teaspoon ground cinnamon

¹/₂ teaspoon ground cardamom

¹/₂ teaspoon smoked paprika

500ml (2 cups) Chicken Broth (see page 24)

1 tablespoon rosewater

juice and grated zest of 1 lime

2 tablespoons honey

150g (1 cup) dried sour cherries

FOR THE JEWELLED RICE:

2 tablespoons olive oil

2 shallots, finely sliced

finely grated zest of 1 orange

300g (1¹/₂ cups) basmati rice

100g (²/₃ cup) raisins

100g (²/₃ cup) dried apricots, finely chopped

600ml (2¹/₂ cups) Vegetable Stock (see page 25)

50g (¹/₂ cup) flaked almonds, toasted

50g (¹/₂ cup) pistachios, roughly chopped

FOR THE CARROTS:

200ml (scant 1 cup) water

200g (scant 1 cup) caster sugar

juice of 1 orange

2 carrots, peeled and cut into long, thin strips

RACK OF LAMB WITH SPRING GREENS, POTATO BAKE AND RED WINE GRAVY

For rack of lamb to be kosher, it must come from the neck end (forequarter), which is slightly smaller than the best end. Even so, this is a wonderful springtime dish, with the moist, garlicky potato, bright greens and tender spring lamb complemented by a rich, intense sauce.

For the potato bake, line a small, deep roasting tray or ovenproof dish (about 30 x 20 x 5cm/12 x 8 x 2 inches) with baking parchment and roughly layer the sliced potatoes in it. Bring the soya cream to the boil with the garlic, thyme, salt and pepper. Remove the thyme and pour the cream over the potatoes. Press the mixture down, cover the tray tightly with foil and bake in an oven preheated to 160°C/325°F/Gas Mark 3 for 45 minutes to 1 hour, until the potatoes are fully cooked (test with a small knife).

Heat the olive oil in a large frying pan. Season the lamb racks, add to the pan and seal over a high heat for 4–5 minutes, until golden brown. Place on a baking tray and roast in an oven preheated to 190°C/375°F/Gas Mark 5 for 12–15 minutes; this should give pink meat. Remove from the oven and allow to rest for 3–4 minutes.

Meanwhile, cook the greens in boiling salted water until tender, then drain well. Heat up the gravy.

Carve each rack of lamb into 3 pieces and serve with the greens and potato bake.

SERVES 4

2 tablespoons olive oil

4 neck-end racks of lamb, each with 4–5 ribs

1 head of spring greens, finely shredded

300ml (1 1/4 cups) Red Wine Gravy (see page 162)

sea salt and black pepper

FOR THE POTATO BAKE:

900g (2 pounds) potatoes, preferably Maris Piper, peeled and finely sliced

500ml (2 cups) soya cream

1 tablespoon crushed garlic

2 sprigs of thyme

1 teaspoon sea salt

1/2 teaspoon black pepper

ROAST CHICKEN WITH POMEGRANATE, WALNUTS AND AUBERGINE RICE

SERVES 4

4 large chicken legs

2 tablespoons pomegranate syrup

2 tablespoons olive oil

100g (1 cup) walnuts, roughly chopped

2 tablespoons honey

400ml (1²/₃ cups) hot Chicken Broth (see page 24)

Aubergine Rice (see page 112)

4 tablespoons fresh pomegranate seeds

sea salt and black pepper

Pomegranate and walnut is a classic combination used by Sephardi Jews in Syria, Iran and Iraq and generally served with poultry. The subtle sweet and sour taste of the pomegranate and honey marries beautifully with the bitter walnut and roasted chicken.

Put the chicken legs in a heavy-based baking tray, about 30 x 20 x 5cm (12 x 8 x 2 inches), and rub with the pomegranate syrup and olive oil. Season with salt and pepper and roast in an oven preheated to 220°C/425°F/Gas Mark 7 for 35–40 minutes, until lightly browned and fully cooked. Remove the chicken from the tray and keep warm.

Then place the tray over a medium heat, add the walnuts and honey and cook for 1 minute. Pour in the hot stock, bring to the boil and simmer for 2 minutes.

To serve, divide the aubergine rice between 4 plates, top with the chicken and pour the sauce around. Garnish with the fresh pomegranate seeds.

LAMB AND APRICOT TAGINE WITH COUSCOUS AND BEETROOT HARISSA

Tagine is a North African speciality, named after the pot it is cooked in. It can be made with meat, fish, vegetables or pulses, and is flavoured with a special spice mix called ras-el-hanout. This literally means 'top of the shop' and there are many variations, each with its own claim for superior flavour and medicinal qualities. In North Africa, lamb is traditionally served on the Seder table for Passover, and couscous is used to stuff whole fish for special Shabbat meals.

Heat 3 tablespoons of the olive oil in a large saucepan, add the diced lamb and fry until nicely browned. Add the onions, carrots, celery, garlic and chillies and fry for 2 minutes, then add all the ground spices. Cook for 3–4 minutes, stirring all the time. Pour in the broth, then add the tomatoes, bay leaves and dried apricots. Bring to the boil, reduce the heat and simmer for 2 hours or until the meat is tender.

Heat the remaining olive oil in a small saucepan, add the couscous and fry gently for 1 minute. Add the hot vegetable stock and cook for 4–5 minutes, stirring all the time, until the couscous has swelled and absorbed the stock. Remove from the heat, cover with a lid and leave to stand for about 5 minutes.

Serve the tagine in warm shallow bows, sprinkled with the coriander and accompanied by the couscous and beetroot harissa.

SERVES 4

5 tablespoons olive oil

800g (1¾ pounds) boned shoulder of lamb, cut into 3cm (1¼-inch) dice

2 onions, cut into 1cm (½-inch) dice

2 carrots, cut into 1cm (½-inch) dice

4 celery sticks, cut into 1cm (½-inch) dice

4 garlic cloves, sliced

2 green chillies, deseeded and finely sliced

1 teaspoon ground cumin

1 teaspoon ground turmeric

½ teaspoon ground cinnamon

½ teaspoon ground nutmeg

½ teaspoon ground fenugreek

½ teaspoon ground cardamom

1 teaspoon smoked paprika

500ml (2 cups) Chicken Broth (see page 24)

400g (1⅔ cups) canned chopped tomatoes

3 bay leaves

150g (3/4 cup) dried apricots, roughly chopped

250g (1½ cups) couscous

250ml (1 cup) hot Vegetable Stock (see page 25)

4 tablespoons coriander leaves

Beetroot Harissa (see page 174), to serve

THAI GREEN CHICKEN CURRY WITH BOK CHOY AND JASMINE RICE

Thai curry paste is usually made with shrimp paste and Thai fish sauce, so could not be considered when cooking meat! I find this kosher version of Thai curry more rustic and fresh tasting, and it still results in a satisfying and fragrant dish.

Heat the groundnut oil in a large saucepan, add the chicken thighs and fry over a high heat until lightly browned all over. Add the onion, lemongrass, chillies, garlic, galangal or ginger and lime leaves and fry for 2 minutes. Add the white wine and simmer until reduced by half, then add the chicken broth and coconut milk and bring to the boil. Simmer for 35–40 minutes, until the chicken is fully cooked.

Meanwhile, steam the jasmine rice and bok choy separately. When the curry is ready, season to taste and serve in warmed bowls with the rice and bok choy, garnished with the basil.

SERVES 4

2 tablespoons groundnut oil

4 large chicken thighs

1 onion, finely diced

2 lemongrass sticks, halved lengthways

3 green chillies, deseeded and finely sliced

1 tablespoon crushed garlic

1 tablespoon minced fresh galangal or ginger root

6 kaffir lime leaves

100ml (scant ½ cup) dry white wine

200ml (scant 1 cup) Chicken Broth (see page 24)

400ml (1 ²/₃cups) coconut milk

300g (1½ cups) jasmine rice

400g (14 ounces) bok choy

a handful of basil leaves

sea salt and white pepper

CORN-FED CHICKEN WITH COURGETTES, MASH AND MUSTARD SAUCE

This is real comfort food: moist roast chicken with soft mash, courgettes, and a mustard sauce to cut through and then marry the flavours together. Courgettes are best in late spring and summer. Choose small, firm, dark green ones, as these have a better flavour and texture and contain more nutrients — especially folic acid and potassium, which are good for your blood pressure and heart.

Heat the olive oil in a large, non-stick frying pan, add the chicken breasts, skin-side down, then add the courgettes. Season with salt and pepper and fry for 5–6 minutes, until golden brown. Reduce the heat slightly and turn the courgettes and chicken over. Fry for about 6–7 minutes, until the courgettes are tender and the chicken is cooked through.

Meanwhile, cook the potatoes in boiling salted water until tender, then drain. Mash with the margarine and season to taste. Gently warm the mustard sauce.

To serve, place a spoonful of mash in the centre of each plate and top with the courgettes and chicken. Spoon the mustard sauce around.

SERVES 4

2 tablespoons olive oil

4 corn-fed chicken breasts, skin on

8 small green courgettes, halved lengthways

800g (1¾ pounds) floury potatoes, preferably Maris Piper, peeled and cut into 2cm (¾-inch) dice

100g (scant ½ cup) Tomor margarine

300ml (1¼ cups) Mustard Sauce (see page 163)

sea salt and black pepper

CONFIT OF DUCK WITH LAVENDER MASH, TOMATO CONFIT AND ROSEMARY JUS

SERVES 4

5 sprigs of rosemary

4 plum tomatoes, skinned, deseeded and cut into quarters

800g (1¾ pounds) floury potatoes, such as Maris Piper, peeled and cut into 2cm (¾-inch) dice

1 teaspoon dried lavender buds

300ml (1¼ cups) Red Wine Gravy (see page 162)

sea salt and black pepper

FOR THE CONFIT OF DUCK:

4 duck legs, well seasoned with sea salt

12 garlic cloves, peeled

½ bunch of thyme

2 bay leaves

12 black peppercorns

400ml (1⅔ cups) melted duck fat (or corn oil)

A dish that contains all the soothing aromas of southern France. The confit produces moist meat that just falls off the bone. It makes an enticing combination with lavender mash and a rosemary-scented sauce.

First dry 4 of the rosemary sprigs by placing them in a very low oven for 2–3 hours or leaving them in a warm place overnight.

For the duck confit, place the duck legs skin-side down in a small, deep roasting tray (about 30 x 20 x 5cm/12 x 8 x 2 inches) with the garlic, thyme, bay leaves and peppercorns. Pour over the melted duck fat so it just covers the legs. Cover the tray tightly with foil, and bake in an oven preheated to 160°C/325°F/Gas Mark 3 for 2½ hours, until the flesh is very tender. Remove from the oven and set aside.

For the tomato confit, brush the tomato quarters with a little of the duck fat and season with sea salt. Place in the hot oven, turn the oven off and leave for 20 minutes, until they are lightly glazed and slightly softened. Meanwhile, cook the potatoes in boiling salted water until tender. Drain well and return to the dry pan. In a small saucepan, heat 3 tablespoons of the duck fat with the lavender buds for 2 minutes. Strain the fat through a fine sieve on to the potatoes and mash well. Bring the gravy to the boil with the fresh rosemary sprig and leave to infuse for 2 minutes.

To serve, fry the duck legs skin-side down in a non-stick frying pan for 6–7 minutes, until brown and crisp. Divide the mash between 4 plates, put the confit duck legs on top and spoon the sauce around. Garnish with the tomato confit and a sprig of dried rosemary.

DUCK SALAD WITH CRISPY NOODLES AND HONEY AND PLUM SAUCE

Oriental food is very popular in modern Jewish communities and this Chinese inspired dish has many subtle combinations: the warm duck, cool salad, sweet and sour sauces, and a rainbow of colours. For an extra touch, you could season the duck with Chinese five-spice powder or spice up the salad with a little fresh chilli.

Heat some oil for deep-frying in a deep-fat fryer or a large deep saucepan. Break the rice noodles in half and deep-fry for about 1 minute, until puffed up and crisp. Remove from the oil, drain on kitchen paper and set aside.

For the sauce, blitz the plums to a smooth purée in a small food processor, then pass through a fine sieve. Mix in the honey and soy sauce and set aside.

Peel the skin from the duck legs and slice it finely. Flake the meat from the bone and fry the meat and skin in a dry non-stick pan until slightly crisp.

Mix the Little Gem lettuce leaves, salad leaves, tomatoes, cucumber, yellow pepper and radishes together in a bowl and toss with the dressing. Divide between 4 plates, scatter with the duck and drizzle with the sauce. Top with the rice noodles and garnish with the coriander sprigs.

SERVES 4

vegetable oil for deep-frying

50g (2 ounces) rice noodles

4 cooked confit duck legs (see page 91)

2 Little Gem lettuces, leaves separated

100g (4 ounces) mixed salad leaves

16 cherry tomatoes, cut in half

1/2 cucumber, halved lengthways, deseeded and sliced

1 yellow pepper, deseeded and finely sliced

4 red radishes, finely sliced

3 tablespoons Honey and Mustard Dressing (see page 166)

4 sprigs of coriander

FOR THE HONEY AND PLUM SAUCE:

2 ripe plums, halved and pitted

2 tablespoons honey

1 tablespoon soy sauce

ROAST DUCK BREASTS WITH CELERIAC MASH, SAVOY CABBAGE AND SAUCE CASSIS

SERVES 4

4 duck breasts

400g (14 ounces) celeriac, peeled and cut into 2cm (³/₄-inch) dice

400g (14 ounces) floury potatoes, preferably Maris Piper, peeled and cut into 2cm (³/₄-inch) dice

½ Savoy cabbage, finely sliced

150ml (²/₃ cup) Vegetable Stock (see page 25)

sea salt and black pepper

FOR THE SAUCE CASSIS:

300ml (1¼ cups) Red Wine Gravy (see page 162)

25ml (2 tablespoons) cassis (blackcurrant liqueur)

75g (½ cup) blackcurrants

Duck with cassis is a classic French combination, with the tartness of the blackcurrant complementing the moist, rich meat. Duck is also enjoyed in the Sephardi world, in a Middle Eastern dish traditionally served with walnuts and pomegranate.

With a small, sharp knife, score the skin on the duck breasts in a criss-cross fashion, cutting through to the fat underneath. Season with salt and pepper. Place the duck breasts skin-side down in a hot non-stick frying pan and fry over a medium heat for about 7–8 minutes, until brown and crisp; the breasts will release some of their fat into the pan. Turn the breasts over and finish cooking for about 5 minutes. Remove from the heat and leave to rest for 3–4 minutes. Meanwhile, cook the celeriac and potatoes together in salted water until tender. Drain well and mash with 2 tablespoons of the duck fat, then season to taste.

Remove the duck breasts from the frying pan and keep warm. Sauté the cabbage in the remaining duck fat over a high heat for 1 minute, then add the vegetable stock and cook for 3–4 minutes, until the liquid has evaporated and the cabbage is tender.

For the sauce, put the gravy, cassis and blackcurrants in a pan and bring to the boil. Taste and adjust the seasoning, if necessary.

To serve, place a portion of mash in the middle of each plate, top with the cabbage and then with the duck. Spoon the sauce around.

VEGETARIAN

VEGETABLE TART WITH WILD ROCKET, PLUM TOMATO AND BALSAMIC VINEGAR SALAD

Although we term this dish in the restaurant as a tart, the flavoursome vegetables here are held together with a light savoury custard, almost like a quiche. It is further enhanced with peppery rocket and a mild balsamic and tomato salad.

Roll out the pastry to 3–4mm (½-inch) thick and use to line a 24cm (9½-inch) loose-bottomed tart tin. Lightly prick the base with a fork and bake for 5 minutes in an oven preheated to 180°C/350°F/Gas Mark 4. Remove from the oven, press the base down gently and set aside.

Heat the olive oil in a pan, add the garlic, onion, courgettes and red pepper and fry gently until lightly browned. Season to taste and leave to cool.

In a bowl, whisk together the eggs and soya cream, then season with salt and pepper. Mix in the cooked vegetables, plus the artichokes and basil. Pour into the pastry case and bake at 180°C/350°F/Gas Mark 4 for 30–35 minutes, until set and nicely browned.

For the salad, mix all the ingredients together and season to taste. Serve the tart warm or cold, with the salad.

SERVES 6

1 quantity of Shortcrust Pastry (see page 156)

2 tablespoons olive oil

1 tablespoon crushed garlic

1 red onion, cut into 1cm (½-inch) dice

2 small green courgettes, cut into 1cm (½-inch) dice

1 red pepper, deseeded and cut into 1cm (½-inch) dice

3 eggs

250ml (1 cup) soya cream

200g (7 ounces) marinated artichoke hearts, cut into quarters

leaves from a bunch of basil, torn

sea salt and black pepper

FOR THE SALAD:

3 tablespoons olive oil

1 tablespoon balsamic vinegar

150g (5 ounces) wild rocket

6 plum tomatoes, cut into 2cm (¾-inch) dice

PUY LENTIL AND BLACK BEAN PICADILLO WITH PIQUILLO PEPPERS AND SAFFRON RICE

Picadillo is a wonderfully rich casserole from South America, traditionally made with beef and garnished with fried plantain. This version includes all the authentic flavours, just without the meat.

Heat the olive oil in a large saucepan, add the onion, garlic and ground cumin and fry over a high heat for 1 minute. Stir in the wine and simmer until reduced by half. Then add the lentils, sweet potato, raisins, olives, lime juice and zest and honey and cook for 5 minutes. Stir in the chopped tomatoes, vegetable stock, bay leaves and capers, bring to the boil and simmer for 45 minutes. Finally stir in the black beans and green pepper and cook for 10–15 minutes.

Serve in warmed shallow bowls, garnished with the piquillo peppers and oregano and accompanied by the saffron rice.

SERVES 4

3 tablespoons olive oil

1 red onion, cut into 2cm (³/₄-inch) dice

4 garlic cloves, finely sliced

1 teaspoon ground cumin

150ml (²/₃ cup) dry white wine

200g (1 cup) Puy lentils, soaked in cold water for 1 hour, then drained

1 sweet potato, peeled and cut into 2cm (³/₄-inch) dice

2 tablespoons raisins

2 tablespoons chopped green olives

juice and grated zest of 1 lime

1 tablespoon honey

400g (1²/₃ cups) canned chopped tomatoes

250ml (1 cup) Vegetable Stock (see page 25)

2 bay leaves

1 tablespoon capers

200g (1 cup) canned black beans, drained

1 green pepper, deseeded and cut into 1cm (¹/₂-inch) dice

100g (4 ounces) canned piquillo peppers, cut into strips

2 tablespoons finely chopped oregano

Saffron Rice (see page 112), to serve

BEAN AND VEGETABLE CASSOULET WITH SMOKED GARLIC MASH AND PESTO

Cassoulet is a traditional stew from Toulouse, which usually includes confit duck or goose, sausage and other meats, plus white beans, wine and herbs. This is a kosher vegetarian version, with a cheese-less pesto.

Heat the olive oil in a large saucepan, add the celeriac and turnips and fry over a high heat until lightly browned. Stir in the leeks, red onions, garlic and mixed herbs and fry for a further 2 minutes. Add the wine, tomatoes and vegetable stock and bring to the boil. Add the bay leaves and simmer for 30 minutes. Finally add the courgettes, yellow pepper and haricot beans and cook for 10–15 minutes. Remove the bay leaves and season to taste.

For the mash, cook the potatoes in boiling salted water until tender, then drain well. Meanwhile, gently fry the smoked garlic in the Tomor for 5–6 minutes. Add the cooked potatoes and mash well. Season to taste.

Serve the cassoulet drizzled with the pesto and accompanied by the mash.

SERVES 4

3 tablespoons olive oil

200g (7 ounces) celeriac, peeled and cut into 2cm (3/4-inch) dice

200g (7 ounces) turnips, peeled and cut into 2cm (3/4-inch) dice

200g (7 ounces) leeks, roughly chopped

2 red onions, cut into 2cm (3/4-inch) dice

4 garlic cloves, finely sliced

1 tablespoon dried mixed herbs

100ml (scant 1/2 cup) dry white wine

400g (1 2/3 cups) canned chopped tomatoes

250ml (1 cup) Vegetable Stock (see page 25)

2 bay leaves

200g (7 ounces) green

courgettes, cut into 1cm (1/2-inch) dice

1 yellow pepper, deseeded and cut into 2cm (3/4-inch) dice

200g (1 cup) canned haricot beans, drained

4 tablespoons Pesto (see page 174)

sea salt and black pepper

FOR THE SMOKED GARLIC MASH:

800g (1 3/4 pounds) floury potatoes, such as Maris Piper, peeled and cut into 2cm (3/4-inch) dice

6 cloves of smoked garlic, roughly chopped

100g (scant 1/2 cup) Tomor margarine

TUSCAN VEGETABLE, RICE AND BEAN SALAD

SERVES 4

100g (½ cup) basmati rice

1 head of radicchio, leaves separated

200g (7 ounces) marinated peppers, roughly chopped

200g (7 ounces) marinated artichokes, cut into quarters

200g (7 ounces) canned borlotti beans, drained

4 plum tomatoes, cut into 2cm (¾-inch) dice

leaves from a bunch of basil, torn

100g (4 ounces) wild rocket

100g (4 ounces) red onions, roughly chopped

200g (7 ounces) marinated grilled aubergines, roughly chopped

1 tablespoon balsamic vinegar

3 tablespoons extra virgin olive oil

4 sprigs of flat-leaf parsley

sea salt and black pepper

This is a quick and easy summer salad inspired by the Tuscan countryside. You could accompany it with some ciabatta croûtons, drizzled with olive oil and baked in a hot oven.

Put the rice in a small pan with 200ml (scant 1 cup) water and a pinch of salt and bring to the boil. Cover and simmer for 10 minutes, until the water has evaporated and the rice is tender. Spread the rice over a small tray and leave to cool.

Divide the radicchio leaves between 4 plates. Combine all the rest of the ingredients except the parsley and season to taste. Place on top of the radicchio leaves and garnish with the parsley.

LINGUINE WITH ROAST TOMATOES, ROCKET, YELLOW PEPPERS AND PESTO

We always like to have a vegetarian pasta dish on the menu and this is one of our favourites – subtle but satisfying, with light, natural flavours and colours.

Place the yellow peppers on a small baking tray, drizzle with 3 tablespoons of the olive oil and season with salt and pepper. Place in an oven preheated to 220°C/425°F/Gas Mark 7 and roast for 20–25 minutes, until slightly blistered. Peel away the skin, deseed the peppers and cut the flesh into strips 1cm (½ inch) wide.

Place the tomatoes on a baking tray, drizzle with the remaining olive oil and season to taste. Roast for 15 minutes, until lightly coloured, then peel away the skin and set the tomatoes aside.

Cook the linguine in boiling salted water until tender, then drain. Return to the pan, add the rocket and mix well. Then carefully fold in the tomatoes, peppers and pesto. Divide between 4 plates and garnish with the basil.

SERVES 4

4 yellow peppers

6 tablespoons olive oil

1kg (2¼ pounds) plum tomatoes, halved lengthways

500g (1 pound 2 ounces) dried linguine

200g (7 ounces) wild rocket

4 tablespoons Pesto (see page 174)

4 sprigs of basil

sea salt and black pepper

PENNE WITH CAPONATA

Caponata is traditionally a cold vegetable stew, served in Sicilian restaurants as an antipasto. Here it is a hot pasta sauce served with penne! Some good bread and a glass of red wine would not be out of place either.

Heat the olive oil in a large saucepan, add the aubergines and fry over a high heat until nicely browned. Add the onions, celery and garlic and fry for 2 minutes. Add the vinegar and honey and cook until reduced by half, then add the tomatoes, olives and capers. Cook over a medium heat for 15 minutes, until thickened, then season to taste.

Cook the pasta in boiling salted water until tender, then drain well. Add to the caponata, divide between 4 plates and sprinkle with the parsley.

SERVES 4–6

4 tablespoons olive oil

2 aubergines, cut into 2cm (3/4-inch) dice

2 red onions, cut into 2cm (3/4-inch) dice

8 celery sticks, sliced

4 garlic cloves, sliced

3 tablespoons white wine vinegar

1 tablespoon honey

400g (1²/₃ cups) canned chopped tomatoes

200g (1¹/₄ cups) black olives, chopped

2 tablespoons capers

500g (1 pound 2 ounces) dried penne

2 tablespoons chopped parsley

sea salt and black pepper

FETTUCCINE WITH PORCINI, RADICCHIO, MARINATED PEPPERS AND OREGANO

SERVES 4

4 tablespoons olive oil

200g (7 ounces) fresh porcini mushrooms, cut into 2cm (³/₄-inch) dice

1 head of radicchio, cut into 2cm (³/₄-inch) dice

250ml (1 cup) Vegetable Stock (see page 25)

200g (7 ounces) marinated peppers, cut into 2cm (³/₄-inch) dice

4 tablespoons finely chopped oregano

juice and grated zest of ¹/₂ lemon

500g (1 pound 2 ounces) fresh fettuccine

sea salt and black pepper

Fettuccine are the original Italian noodles. The soft, golden ribbons are complemented beautifully by the king of mushrooms – porcini (cep in French or penny bun in English). This wild mushroom is considered the best for flavour, texture and versatility. It can carry other ingredients very well, without being dominated by them.

Heat the olive oil in a large saucepan, add the mushrooms and fry over a high heat until nicely browned. Add the radicchio and vegetable stock and simmer until the stock is reduced by half. Stir in the peppers, oregano and lemon juice and zest, then season to taste.

Cook the pasta in boiling salted water until tender, then drain. Mix with the sauce and serve in warmed shallow bowls.

POTATO AND THYME GNOCCHI WITH PAPRIKA SAUCE AND BLACK OLIVES

Gnocchi are little poached or baked dumplings from Italy. These delightfully light mouthfuls could also be made with basil and served with a fresh tomato sauce.

Bake the potatoes in an oven preheated to 200°C/400°F/Gas Mark 6 until tender. Cut them in half and scoop out the flesh into a mixing bowl. While it is still hot, add the flour, polenta, egg and thyme and mix well with a wooden spoon to form a smooth dough. Leave to cool for 10 minutes, then use a teaspoon to scoop out pieces of dough. Gently roll each one out on a floured board with the palm of your hand to make an oval shape. Cook the gnocchi in a large pan of boiling salted water until they rise to the surface, then drain well in a colander.

Gently heat the paprika sauce and divide between 4 shallow bowls. Top with the gnocchi and scatter over the chopped olives.

SERVES 4

750g (1 pound 10 ounces) floury potatoes, such as Maris Piper

100g ($^2/_3$ cup) plain flour

50g ($^1/_3$ cup) instant polenta

1 egg

2 tablespoons fresh thyme leaves, finely chopped

500ml (2 cups) Paprika Sauce (see page 168)

4 tablespoons roughly chopped black olives

SIDE DISHES

HOME-MADE CHIPS

There's nothing like the great British chip. Universally loved, it can be served with almost anything – and occasionally sprinkled with vinegar, to the bemusement of foreigners, who normally only see the smaller frites accompanied with ketchup or mayonnaise.

This recipe shows how chips should be prepared in order to be appreciated properly (not just cut up and thrown in the fryer). If you can find them, do use Binjte potatoes, as they are superb for chips, although Maris Pipers are good all-rounders.

Peel the potatoes and cut them into slices 1.5cm (½-inch) thick. Then cut the slices into 1.5cm (½-inch) strips and wash under cold running water to remove excess starch. Pat dry with a tea towel.

Heat the oil to 115°C/230°F in a deep-fat fryer, add the chips and fry for 8–10 minutes, until fully cooked but not coloured – do this in batches so as not to overcrowd the pan. Remove and drain on kitchen paper. Spread the chips out on a tray, allow to cool, then chill, preferably overnight. To serve, deep-fry the chips at 180°C/350°F until golden brown, then drain on kitchen paper. Season with sea salt.

SERVES 4

1kg (2¼ pounds) Binje or
 Maris Piper potatoes
vegetable oil for deep-frying
sea salt

DILL AND HORSERADISH LATKES

MAKES 12

2 large potatoes, weighing about 700g (1½ pounds), peeled and grated

1 onion, weighing about 150g (5 ounces), peeled and grated

3 tablespoons plain flour

1 teaspoon baking powder

1 egg

1 egg yolk

½ teaspoon salt

½ teaspoon ground white pepper

2 tablespoons chopped dill

2 tablespoons finely grated horseradish

4 tablespoons olive oil

Latkes are small potato fritters, similar to Swiss rösti. Traditionally served at Hanukah, the Jewish Festival of Lights, they can be eaten as a side dish or as part of a starter – for example, with Matjes Herring with Apple and Red Onion (see page 45).

Put the grated potato in a colander and wash under cold running water to remove the excess starch. Pat dry, place in a mixing bowl and add all the remaining ingredients except the olive oil. Mix until well combined. Squeeze out any excess liquid and then divide the mixture into 12 pieces on a chopping board. Pat each piece into a small, flat disc. Heat the olive oil in a large frying pan and fry the latkes for about 2 minutes on each side, until lightly browned. Place on a baking sheet and bake in an oven preheated to 180°C/350°F/Gas Mark 4 for 4–5 minutes, until fully cooked.

SAFFRON RICE

A colourful, subtly flavoured pilau, which goes well with a variety of Mediterranean and Middle Eastern dishes.

Heat the olive oil in a saucepan, add the saffron and fry for 1 minute. Add the shallots and rice and fry for 2 minutes, stirring all the time. Add the hot vegetable stock, a good pinch of sea salt and some pepper, then cover and cook for 10–12 minutes, stirring occasionally, until all the liquid has been absorbed and the rice is tender.

SERVES 4

2 tablespoons olive oil

1g (a large pinch) saffron strands

2 shallots, finely diced

300g (1½ cups) basmati rice

600ml (2½ cups) hot Vegetable Stock (see page 25)

sea salt and white pepper

AUBERGINE RICE

This popular Turkish pilau is usually served with grilled meats, fish and vegetable casseroles.

Heat the olive oil in a saucepan, add the aubergine and fry over a high heat until lightly browned. Add the onion and fry for 2 minutes, then add the rice and mix well. Pour in the hot stock, lower the heat and cook, covered, for 10–12 minutes, stirring occasionally, until all the liquid has been absorbed and the rice is tender. Season to taste and serve.

SERVES 4

3 tablespoons olive oil

1 large aubergine, cut into 1cm (½-inch) dice

1 onion, finely chopped

200g (1 cup) basmati rice

400ml (1⅔ cups) hot Vegetable Stock (see page 25)

sea salt and black pepper

CABBAGE, CARAWAY AND SMOKED BEEF

SERVES 4

2 tablespoons groundnut oil

75g (3 ounces) smoked beef, finely shredded

1 red onion, finely diced

1 teaspoon caraway seeds

1/2 white cabbage, finely shredded

250ml (1 cup) Vegetable Stock (see page 25)

sea salt and black pepper

This is a central European classic, typically served with braised or boiled meats. It goes very well with new potatoes.

Heat the groundnut oil in a large saucepan, add the smoked beef and onion and fry over a high heat until the onion browns slightly. Add the caraway seeds and cabbage, stir well and cook for 3–4 minutes, until the cabbage begins to soften. Pour in the stock and cover with a lid. Cook for 5–6 minutes, until all the stock has been absorbed, then season to taste.

BRAISED CELERY AND ORANGE

SERVES 4

1 tablespoon groundnut oil

2 shallots, finely diced

12 celery sticks, sliced

100ml (scant 1/2 cup) dry white wine

200ml (scant 1/2 cup) orange juice

sea salt and black pepper

A lovely dish to accompany fish or chicken. You could garnish it with orange segments and snipped chives.

Heat the groundnut oil in a saucepan, add the shallots and celery and fry over a medium heat for 2 minutes without colouring. Add the wine and simmer until reduced by half. Pour in the orange juice and simmer for 10–15 minutes, until almost evaporated. Season to taste and serve.

HONEY-ROASTED VEGETABLES

A hearty autumn vegetable dish, which goes well with any roast fowl.

Peel the vegetables and cut them into 2cm (¾-inch) dice. Spread them out on a baking tray lined with baking parchment, drizzle with the olive oil and season with salt and pepper. Bake in an oven preheated to 190°C/375°F/Gas Mark 5 for 20 minutes, then drizzle over the honey and bake for 5 minutes longer, until lightly browned. Serve scattered with the thyme.

SERVES 4

200g (7 ounces) celeriac
200g (7 ounces) beetroot
200g (7 ounces) swede
200g (7 ounces) carrots
3 tablespoons olive oil
3 tablespoons honey
1 tablespoon chopped thyme
sea salt and black pepper

BROCCOLI WITH SESAME AND SOY

An oriental classic, and our most popular side order in the restaurant. You could add some finely sliced red chilli to give a bit of extra colour and bite.

Steam the broccoli for 3–4 minutes, until just tender, then place in a serving dish. Spoon over the soy sauce and sesame oil and sprinkle with the sesame seeds.

SERVES 4

400g (14 ounces) broccoli florets
3 tablespoons soy sauce
3 tablespoons sesame oil
1 tablespoon sesame seeds

LITTLE GEMS WITH ENGLISH DRESSING

An English classic, somewhat forgotten, and on the scene long before the famous Caesar salad. Like its modern cousin, this salad could be served garnished with warm croûtons.

Put all the ingredients for the dressing in a bowl and whisk until completely emulsified. Toss the lettuce leaves in the dressing, place in a serving bowl and sprinkle with the chives.

SERVES 4

4 Little Gem lettuces, leaves separated

2 tablespoons snipped chives

FOR THE DRESSING:

½ teaspoon English mustard

1 teaspoon crushed garlic

1 teaspoon Worcestershire sauce

1 teaspoon anchovy essence

4 tablespoons mayonnaise

1 teaspoon white wine vinegar

1 tablespoon cold water

sea salt and black pepper

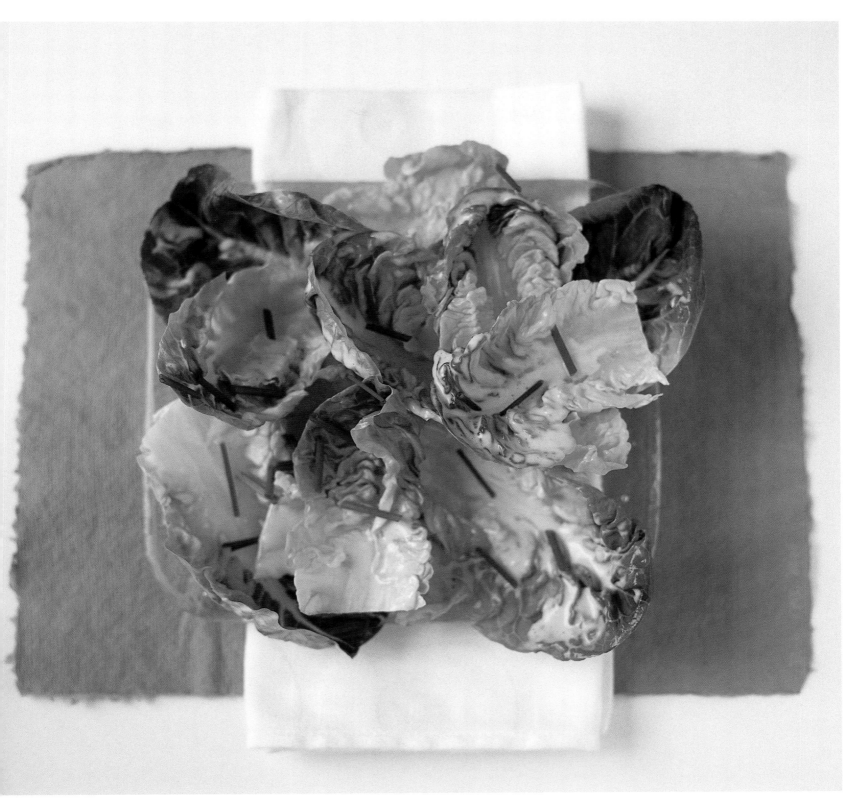

SWEET PEPPERS WITH BLACK BEAN SAUCE

An interesting oriental side dish, which would accompany steamed rice or braised chicken extremely well.

Heat the oil in a wok or large frying pan, add the peppers and stir-fry for 2 minutes. Add the black beans, shallots and garlic and stir-fry for 1 minute, then add the soy sauce, honey and vegetable stock. Simmer for 4–5 minutes, until almost all the liquid has evaporated. Serve immediately.

SERVES 4

2 tablespoons groundnut oil

2 red peppers, deseeded and cut into 2cm (³/₄-inch) dice

1 green pepper, deseeded and cut into 2cm (³/₄-inch) dice

1 yellow pepper, deseeded and cut into 2cm (³/₄-inch) dice

3 tablespoons cooked black beans, roughly chopped

4 shallots, finely diced

4 garlic cloves, finely diced

3 tablespoons soy sauce

1 tablespoon honey

125ml (¹/₂ cup) Vegetable Stock (see page 25)

SWEET POTATO MASH WITH CUMIN

Baking sweet potatoes in their skins enhances their natural sweetness, while cumin really brings out the flavour.

Arrange the potatoes on a bed of salt in a baking tray and bake in an oven preheated to 200°C/400°F/Gas Mark 6 for about 45 minutes, until slightly blistered and soft to the touch. Allow to cool for 10 minutes, then peel. Heat the olive oil in a saucepan, add the cumin and fry gently for 1 minute. Add the potato flesh, beat well and cook for 3–4 minutes over a low heat to remove excess moisture. Season to taste and serve.

SERVES 4

1kg (2¹/₂ pounds) large sweet potatoes

2 tablespoons olive oil

1 teaspoon ground cumin

sea salt and black pepper

TZIMMES

Tzimmes can be any meat or vegetable dish sweetened with sugar and honey, but to most Ashkenazi it refers to glazed carrots – and very sweet ones at that! This is usually served as an accompaniment to meat.

Combine all the ingredients except the honey in a saucepan and bring to the boil, stirring to dissolve the sugar. Simmer for 1 hour, until the carrots are soft and translucent. Remove the cinnamon stick, drain off the syrup and mix in the honey.

SERVES 4

600g (1 pound 5 ounces) carrots, finely sliced

1 cinnamon stick

juice and grated zest of 1 orange

350g (1½ cups) caster sugar

75g (½ cup) raisins

2 tablespoons honey

SPÄTZLE

These traditional Germanic fresh egg noodles may require a bit of hard work on the arm but it is well worth it! Serve with Braised Beefsteak (see page 78).

Put all the ingredients in a large bowl and mix together with your hand to make a soft, sticky dough. Then beat the dough with your hand until it begins to leave the side of the bowl; this will take about 5 minutes. Place a quarter of the mixture at a time on a chopping board and use a large chopping knife to scrape fine strips of dough into a large pan of boiling salted water (about 3 litres/12 cups). As the pasta floats to the surface, remove with a slotted spoon. Serve immediately.

SERVES 4

300g (2 cups) plain flour

6 eggs

1 teaspoon vegetable oil

1 teaspoon cold water

½ teaspoon ground nutmeg

½ teaspoon fine sea salt

½ teaspoon ground white pepper

KASHA AND RED ONION PILAU

Kasha, or roasted buckwheat, is a central and northern European speciality with a malty flavour that is quite an acquired taste. It is traditionally served with wild mushrooms or various meat dishes.

Heat the oil in a saucepan, add the onion and fry over a high heat for 2 minutes. Add the kasha and stir well, then pour in the hot stock. Bring to the boil and simmer, covered, for 15–20 minutes, until the kasha is tender and all the stock has been absorbed. Season to taste.

SERVES 4

2 tablespoons groundnut oil

1 red onion, finely diced

200g (1 heaping cup) kasha (roasted buckwheat)

500ml (2 cups) hot Chicken Broth (see page 24)

sea salt and black pepper

PEA AND SWEETCORN BULGAR PILAU

A lovely, fresh-tasting pilau, which goes very well with whole grilled or baked fish.

Heat the olive oil in a saucepan, add the shallots and fry over a high heat for 1 minute. Then add the peas, sweetcorn and bulgar and mix well. Pour in the hot stock and simmer for 8–10 minutes, stirring occasionally, until all the liquid has been absorbed. Remove from the heat, cover with a lid and leave for 5 minutes, so the bulgar will finish cooking in its own steam.

SERVES 4

3 tablespoons olive oil

2 shallots, finely diced

100g (^{2}/$_3$ cup) fresh peas

100g (1 cup) sweetcorn kernels

200g (1 heaping cup) bulgar (fine cracked wheat)

400ml (1^2/$_3$ cups) hot Vegetable Stock (see page 25)

DESSERTS

VANILLA AND PEACH CRÈME BRÛLÉE WITH RASPBERRIES AND ALMOND BRANDY SNAPS

This crème brûlée is a take on the Escoffier classic, peach melba, which combines poached peaches with vanilla ice cream, toasted almonds and raspberry sauce. Whichever way it is conceived, the combination is timeless and brilliant.

Divide the peaches between 6 ramekins, 175–200ml (¾ cup) in capacity, and set aside. Put the soya milk, soya cream, vanilla pod and its seeds in a small saucepan and bring to the boil. Remove from the heat and leave to infuse for 5 minutes. Whisk the egg yolks and caster sugar together, pour in the milk mixture, whisking all the time, then remove the vanilla pod. Mix well and pour into the ramekins.

Place the ramekins in a baking tray half filled with cold water and bake in an oven preheated to 140°C/275°F/Gas Mark 1 for 35 minutes, until only slightly set. Leave to cool, then chill until set. Finally sprinkle with the demerara sugar and glaze with a blowtorch or under a very hot grill.

Mix the raspberries with the raspberry coulis. Serve the brûlées accompanied by the brandy snaps and with the sauce in a jug.

SERVES 6

3 ripe peaches, skinned, pitted and cut into 1cm dice

250ml (1 cup) soya milk

250ml (1 cup) soya cream

1 vanilla pod, split in half lengthways and seeds removed

150g (5 ounces) egg yolks (about 4–5)

150g (⅔ cup) caster sugar

100g (½ cup) demerara sugar

100g (½ cup) raspberries

100ml (scant ½ cup) Raspberry Coulis (see page 171)

12 Almond Brandy Snaps (see page 157)

FRANGIPANE AND ELDERBERRY TART WITH ELDERFLOWER ICE CREAM

SERVES 8

½ quantity of Sweet Pastry (see page 157)

200g (1¾ cups) ground almonds

200g (2 cups) icing sugar

200g (scant 1 cup) Tomor margarine, softened

3 large eggs, lightly beaten

100g (½ cup) fresh elderberries

25ml (5 teaspoons) Amaretto liqueur

4 tablespoons flaked almonds

Elderflower Ice Cream (see page 146)

Raspberry Coulis (see page 171)

This is similar to a Bakewell tart, with the elderberries replacing the raspberry jam but still with the wonderfully moist almond frangipane sponge. Elderberries are a seasonal fruit, with the elder tree bearing ripe berries from September through to early October. They make great jellies, jam and wine.

Roll the pastry out on a lightly floured board to 3mm (⅛-inch) thick and use to line a lightly greased loose-bottomed 24cm (9½-inch) tart tin, 3cm (1¼-inches) deep. Chill while you prepare the filling.

For the frangipane, mix the almonds, icing sugar and margarine to a fine paste. Slowly add the eggs, keeping the mixture smooth. Then carefully fold in the berries and Amaretto. Pour into the pastry case, level the top and sprinkle with the flaked almonds. Bake in an oven preheated to 160°C/325°F/Gas Mark 3 for 30–35 minutes, until golden brown. Serve each portion with a scoop of ice cream and a tablespoon of coulis.

PEAR AND FIG TARTE TATIN WITH PRUNE AND COGNAC ICE CREAM

Tarte tatin is the classic French upside-down tart, traditionally made with apples and served with vanilla ice cream. You will need 6 individual Tatin tins, about 10cm (4 inches) in diameter, for this recipe. Alternatively you could make one large tart in a 20–24cm (8–9½-inch) baking tin.

Roll out the pastry on a lightly floured surface to about 3mm (⅛ inch) thick, then cut it into six 10cm (4-inch) rounds with a plain cutter.

Put the sugar and lime juice in a small, heavy-based saucepan and heat gently, stirring until the sugar has dissolved. Raise the heat and boil without stirring until it turns into a pale golden caramel. Divide the caramel between the 6 Tatin tins. Layer the slices of pear on top of the caramel, completely covering the base of the tins.

Layer the fig slices over the pear and then top with the puff pastry discs, pressing them down well. Bake in an oven preheated to 190°C/375°F/Gas Mark 5 for 15 minutes or until the pastry is golden brown. Allow to cool slightly, then invert each tart on to a serving plate, top with a ball of ice cream and drizzle with the sauce.

SERVES 6

200g (7 ounces) puff pastry

200g (scant 1 cup) caster sugar

juice of 1 lime

6 firm pears, peeled, cored and sliced

6 large figs, each cut into 6 slices

Prune and Cognac Ice Cream (see page 146)

6 tablespoons Orange and Pomegranate Sauce (see page 170)

LOCKSHEN PUDDING WITH ICE CREAM AND APPLE COULIS

Lockshen pudding is the traditional Ashkenazi dessert, made by Jewish communities in central Europe since the Middle Ages. The name derives from the Polish word for noodles, lokszyn, which are similiar to spätzle (see page 120). However, this recipe uses the Italian egg pasta, taglierini, which produces a lighter and softer pudding.

Cook the pasta in a large pan of unsalted boiling water, then drain in a colander. Return the pasta to the pan and stir in the margarine until melted. Add the ground spices, mixed peel, raisins, lemon juice and zest and mix well.

In a separate bowl, whisk the eggs and sugar together until thick and creamy, add the grated apples and vanilla extract and mix well. Pour on to the pasta mix and fold through until fully combined. Pour the mixture into a small roasting tin (about 30 x 20 x 4cm/12 x 8 x 1½ inches) lined with baking parchment and spread evenly. Cover with another piece of baking parchment and bake in an oven preheated to 190°C/375°F/Gas Mark 5 for 35 minutes, until nicely browned and set. Turn out on to a chopping board and cut into squares or rounds (using a pastry cutter). Serve with the ice cream and apple coulis.

SERVES 6

250g (9 ounces) taglierini

150g (2/3 cup) Tomor margarine

2 tablespoons ground cinnamon

1 tablespoon ground mixed spice

100g (4 ounces) candied mixed peel

150g (scant 1 cup) raisins

juice and grated zest of 1 lemon

4 large eggs

225g (1 cup) caster sugar

3 Granny Smith apples, cored and grated

25ml (5 teaspoons) natural vanilla extract

Vanilla Ice Cream (see page 146)

Apple Coulis (see page 171)

CHOCOLATE BROWNIES WITH PISTACHIO ANGLAISE AND WHITE CHOCOLATE AND RASPBERRY ICE CREAM

This is a soft, pudding-style chocolate brownie, dark and decadent! So it needs a little care, patience and attention. Each portion must be warmed up on its serving plate so that it holds its shape, but it's well worth the time and effort. Here the brownies are served with pistachio and raspberry – chocolate's perfect partners.

Put the chocolate and margarine in a bowl set over a pan of simmering water, making sure the water isn't touching the bowl. Leave until melted, then set aside.

In a separate bowl, whisk together the eggs and sugar until pale and doubled in volume. Add the vanilla extract and then fold in the chocolate mixture. Combine the flour, baking powder and salt, then fold them gradually into the chocolate mixture until fully combined. Add the walnuts. Pour the mixture into a small baking tray (about 30 x 20 x 4cm/12 x 8 x 1½ inches) lined with baking parchment. Bake in an oven preheated to 180°C/350°F/Gas Mark 4 for 20 minutes; do not over bake – the brownie will be very light and soft. Allow to cool, then chill for 4–5 hours or overnight, until completely set.

Remove the brownie from the fridge and trim away the edges. Cut into portions and place each portion on a plate. Microwave individually for 30 seconds, so the brownie is warm and oozing. Serve with the pistachio anglaise and a ball of ice cream.

SERVES 6–8

300g (11 ounces) kosher chocolate (70 per cent cocoa solids), finely chopped

150g (⅔ cup) Tomor margarine, cut into 1cm (½-inch) dice

6 large eggs

500g (2 cups) caster sugar

25ml (5 teaspoons) natural vanilla extract

225g (1⅔ cups) plain flour

1 tablespoon baking powder

½ teaspoon salt

150g (1⅓ cups) walnuts, roughly chopped

White Chocolate and Raspberry Ice Cream (see page 146)

Pistachio Anglaise (see page 169)

APPLE AND BLACKBERRY CRUMBLE WITH CINNAMON ICE CREAM AND SAUCE ANGLAISE

Fruit crumble, the quintessential British dessert, with a proper egg custard, is pure comfort food. In the restaurant we serve the crumble and ice cream in separate ramekins and the sauce in individual jugs – though it looks just as good spooned from a pie dish, with a pool of sauce and a scoop of ice cream!

Melt 25g (2 tablespoons) of the margarine in a saucepan over a low heat, add the apples and honey and cook for about 8 minutes, until the apples begin to soften. Remove from the heat, stir in the blackberries and divide the mixture between four 200ml ($^7/_8$ cup) ramekins (or put it in a medium pie dish).

To make the crumble, cut the remaining margarine into 1cm ($^1/_2$-inch) dice and rub it into the flour between your fingers and thumbs until the mixture resembles rough breadcrumbs. Then fold in the caster sugar and sprinkle the crumble mixture over the fruit. Bake in an oven preheated to 220°C/425°F/Gas Mark 7 for 15 minutes, until golden brown. Serve with the warmed sauce anglaise and the cinnamon ice cream.

SERVES 4

150g ($^2/_3$ cup) Tomor margarine

4 Granny Smith apples, peeled, cored and cut into 1cm ($^1/_2$-inch) dice

2 tablespoons honey

150g ($^2/_3$ cup) blackberries

200g (1$^1/_3$ cups) plain flour

125g ($^1/_2$ cup) caster sugar

Sauce Anglaise (see page 169)

Cinnamon Ice Cream (see page 146)

STRAWBERRY AND SHORTBREAD TART WITH BLACK PEPPER ICE CREAM AND SWEET BALSAMIC SAUCE

SERVES 8

250ml (1 cup) soya cream

100ml (scant ½ cup) soya milk

1 tablespoon natural vanilla extract

3 egg yolks

100g (scant ½ cup) caster sugar

25g (⅙ cup) plain flour

250g (1⅔ cups) strawberries, hulled and quartered

Black Pepper Ice Cream (see page 146)

Sweet Balsamic Sauce (see page 168)

icing sugar for dusting

FOR THE SHORTBREAD:

375g (2½ cups) plain flour

a pinch of salt

50g (½ cup) cornmeal or fine polenta

200g (scant 1 cup) caster sugar

200g (scant 1 cup) Tomor margarine, cut into 1cm (½-inch) dice

2 eggs

juice of 1 lime

This dessert combines two ideas: a Celtic shortbread and pastry cream tart, similar to the Iberian pastel vasco, and the Italian tradition of serving new-season strawberries seasoned with freshly milled black pepper and drizzled with sweetened balsamic vinegar – or, for the more discerning gourmet, an aged 10-year-old balsamic with a natural sweetness and low acidity.

Put the soya cream, milk and vanilla in a saucepan, place over a low heat and bring to simmering point. Meanwhile, in a bowl whisk together the egg yolks, caster sugar and flour until smooth. Pour on the hot liquid and whisk well. Return to the cleaned-out saucepan and cook over a low heat for at least 5 minutes, whisking occasionally, until the mixture has thickened nicely and the taste of the flour has cooked out. Remove from the heat, fold in the strawberries and leave to cool.

For the shortbread, sift the flour, salt, cornmeal and caster sugar into a bowl. Rub in the margarine until the mixture resembles breadcrumbs. Separate one of the eggs and mix the yolk with the remaining egg and the lime juice. Pour them into the flour mixture and stir to form a smooth, soft dough. Cut the dough in half, wrap in cling film and chill for 30 minutes.

Roll out both pieces of dough to a thickness of 3mm (⅛-inch), dusting with flour to prevent sticking, if necessary. Use one piece to line a 25cm (10-inch) loose-bottomed tart tin, 3cm (1¼ inches) deep. Fill the tart with the strawberry pastry cream, brush the pastry edges with the egg white and top with the second piece of pastry, trimming it to fit (you could save the trimmings to make shortbread biscuits). Place in an oven preheated to 180°C/350°F/Gas Mark 4 and bake for 30–35 minutes, until golden brown. Leave to cool for 30 minutes before slicing. Serve each portion with a ball of ice cream, drizzled with sweet balsamic sauce and dusted with icing sugar.

ZWETSCHGEN DATSCHI WITH CINNAMON ICE CREAM AND ORANGE SAUCE

Zwetschgen datschi is a classic Germanic flat, yeasted pastry, topped with plums and eaten as an accompaniment to mid-morning coffee or as a dessert. It is best to use ripe, late-summer plums, which will hold their juice and release their full aroma upon baking. You could also sprinkle this tart with some crumble (see page 134) before baking, for extra texture.

Dissolve the dried yeast in the warm soya milk and leave to stand for 10 minutes. Put the flour in a mixing bowl and make a well in the centre. Add the yeast mixture, egg, margarine, honey and salt to the well. Gradually draw the flour into the liquid and mix until a smooth dough is achieved. Turn out on to a lightly floured surface and knead for 5–10 minutes, until smooth and elastic. Return to the bowl, cover with a tea towel and leave in a warm place for 30 minutes or until the dough has doubled in size.

Remove the dough from the bowl and place on a work surface dusted with flour. Knock the dough back to its original size and then roll out to a thickness of 5mm (¼-inch), dusting with extra flour to prevent sticking, if necessary. Use the dough to line a 25cm (10-inch) loose-bottomed tart tin and arrange the plum wedges on top in a spiral pattern. Leave to prove in a warm place for 20 minutes.

Bake the tart in an oven preheated to 190°C/375°F/Gas Mark 5 for 20–25 minutes, until the pastry is golden brown. Remove from the oven and sprinkle with a mixture of the ground cinnamon and caster sugar. Cut into wedges and serve each portion drizzled with the sauce and accompanied by the cinnamon ice cream.

SERVES 6

1 teaspoon dried yeast

125ml (½ cup) soya milk, warmed

250g (1⅔ cups) plain flour

½ egg, whisked

50g (4 tablespoons) Tomor margarine, melted

1 tablespoon honey

a pinch of salt

750g (1 pound 10 ounces) ripe plums, pitted and cut into 8 wedges each

4 tablespoons caster sugar

1 teaspoon ground cinnamon

Orange and Pomegranate Sauce (see page 170)

Cinnamon Ice Cream (see page 146)

SUMMER BERRY GRUETZE WITH SAUCE ANGLAISE AND LAVENDER SHORTBREAD

A gruetze is a soft, half-set fruit and wine jelly, traditionally served with vanilla custard. I have given this central European dessert a British accent with the addition of a comforting Lavender Shortbread.

Put the wine, juice and sugar in a saucepan, bring to the boil and whisk in the gelatine. Remove from the heat and allow to cool for 5 minutes. Add the berries to the warm liquid and then divide between 4 dessert or wine glasses, leaving at least 1cm (½-inch) of space at the top. Chill for 4–5 hours or overnight.

To serve, gently spoon the chilled Sauce Anglaise on top of the gruetze and accompany with the lavender shortbread.

SERVES 4

250ml (1 cup) Kiddush wine

250ml (1 cup) cranberry juice

150g (⅔ cup) caster sugar

10g (⅓ ounce) kosher gelatine

150g (⅔ cup) blueberries

150g (⅔ cup) raspberries

100g (½ cup) redcurrants

200g (1⅓ cups) strawberries, hulled and quartered

300ml (1¼ cups) Sauce Anglaise (see page 169), chilled

Lavender Shortbread (see page 158), to serve

BAKED HONEY AND HAZELNUT PEARS WITH AMARETTO ICE CREAM AND CHOCOLATE SAUCE

Poached pears have a great affinity with chocolate, and also with nuts such as hazelnut, almond and pistachio. When baked with wine and honey, they acquire an extra richness. With its wonderful shiny glaze, this makes an indulgent dessert for an autumn evening.

Core each pear from the bottom with an apple corer or small knife, being careful not to dislodge the stalk from the top. Carefully peel the pears. Next, combine the hazelnuts, dates, jam and vanilla to make a paste and stuff the pears with this mixture. Grease a small, deep roasting tin with the margarine and stand the pears upright in it.

Bring the honey, apple juice, wine and allspice berries to the boil in a small saucepan and carefully pour them over the pears. Cover the tin tightly with foil and place in an oven preheated to 180°C/350°F/Gas Mark 4. Bake for 40–45 minutes, until the pears are just tender. Serve warm, with a ball of Amaretto ice cream and a pool of chocolate sauce.

SERVES 6

6 firm pears

100g (1 cup) ground hazelnuts

2 dates, finely chopped

1 tablespoon raspberry jam

1 teaspoon natural vanilla extract

50g (4 tablespoons) Tomor margarine

200ml (scant 1 cup) honey

200ml (scant 1 cup) apple juice

200ml (scant 1 cup) dry white wine

4 allspice berries

Amaretto Ice Cream (see page 146)

Chocolate Sauce (see page 170)

MARINATED CHERRIES WITH BASIL ICE CREAM AND CHOCOLATE LATTICE

SERVES 4

500g (1 pound 2 ounces) fresh cherries, pitted

100ml (scant 1/2 cup) cherry brandy

1 tablespoon caster sugar

50g (2 ounces) kosher dark chocolate, melted

Basil Ice Cream (see page 148)

Cherries are a summer treat in Britain, at their best during July, but they have a much longer season in America and southern Europe. Chocolate has been considered an ideal partner for cherries for many years, but basil? Surprisingly, it works well with both!

Combine the cherries, cherry brandy and sugar in a small container. Cover with a lid and chill for a couple of hours or, better still, overnight.

For the lattice, line a small tray with baking parchment and drizzle the melted chocolate over it with a teaspoon, using a quick zigzag motion one way and then the next to create a fine crisscross pattern. Repeat to make 4 lattices. Place in the fridge to cool and set.

To serve, divide the cherries and their marinade between 4 small bowls or dessert glasses. Top with a ball of basil ice cream and place a chocolate lattice on top of that.

ALMOND BLANCMANGE WITH WATERMELON GRANITA

This dessert has echoes of the Mediterranean, with the chilled almond milk pudding of southern Spain and the diamond-like frozen water ice of Sicily, topped with chocolate chips to resemble the missing pips. It's visually stunning and the flavours are elegant and subtle. You could also accompany the granita with Rosewater Macaroons (see page 158).

For the blancmange, put the soya milk, Amaretto and 75g (1/3 cup) of the caster sugar in a saucepan and bring to simmering point. Whisk in the gelatine until dissolved, then remove from the heat and leave to cool. Divide the mixture between 4 martini or dessert glasses (each glass should be about half full) and chill for 3–4 hours, until set.

For the granita, purée the watermelon flesh, grenadine syrup and the remaining caster sugar in a food processor. Transfer to a large tray or shallow container and place in the freezer. Scrape the mixture with a fork every half hour as it freezes so it forms large crystals. After about 3 hours, the entire mixture should be crystallised.

To serve, spoon the granita on top of the set blancmange and garnish with the chocolate chips and a sprig of mint.

SERVES 4

450ml (scant 2 cups) soya milk

50ml (3 tablespoons) Amaretto liqueur

150g (2/3 cup) caster sugar

5g (1/4 ounce) kosher gelatine

250g (9 ounces) watermelon flesh, minus the pips

25ml (5 teaspoons) grenadine syrup

1 tablespoon kosher chocolate chips

4 sprigs of mint

KAZANDIBI WITH SPICED FIG ICE CREAM AND ORANGE SALAD

SERVES 6

150g (5 ounces) skinless, boneless chicken breast

750ml (3 cups) soya milk

250ml (1 cup) soya cream

175g (³/₄ cup) caster sugar

a pinch of salt

3 tablespoons cornflour

1¹/₂ tablespoons rosewater

4 tablespoons demerara sugar

4 oranges, peeled and segmented

1 tablespoon finely chopped mint

Spiced Fig Ice Cream (see page 175)

Kazandibi is a speciality of Istanbul, the gateway between East and West. Don't be put off by the inclusion of chicken in a dessert, as it gives this dish a wonderful texture and mild, virtually undetectable flavour.

Traditionally kazandibi is cooked on the stove in deep trays until caramelised on the bottom, then cut and rolled up. Here, however, it is served in ramekins and brûléed – a rather more dainty and westernised method!

Put the chicken breast in a small saucepan, cover with water and bring to the boil. Simmer for 10–12 minutes, until fully cooked, then drain and rinse with cold water. Pat dry and shred along the grain with your fingers into fine strips. Divide between six 200ml (⁷/₈ cup) ramekins and set aside.

Put the soya milk, cream, caster sugar and salt in a saucepan and bring gently to the boil. In a cup, mix the cornflour and rosewater together. Whisk them into the hot milk and cook until it begins to thicken. Divide the mixture between the ramekins and leave to cool for 30 minutes, then chill for 2–3 hours, until set.

To serve, sprinkle the demerara sugar on top and glaze with a blowtorch or place under a very hot grill until lightly caramelised. Serve with the ice cream and the orange segments sprinkled with the chopped mint.

DAIRY FREE SOYA MILK ICE CREAM

When I started working at Bevis Marks, I realised that making a truly palatable kosher, non-dairy ice cream was going to be a challenge.

The only alternative to fresh milk and double cream seemed to be an artificially sweetened and thickened kosher dessert cream. So Kenny and I went hunting and eventually sourced a thin, mild-tasting soya cream and a wonderful Japanese soya milk. I started to experiment with these, initially making a thin custard that I chilled and churned with a little cream. This mixture didn't freeze properly and tasted disappointingly like most commercial soya-based desserts. The solution was to use more egg and sugar to give the custard extra body, a higher proportion of soya cream to stabilise the mixture, and stronger flavours to combat the soya taste. Once I mixed the cream and custard together before churning, the mixture froze successfully. So we finally cracked it! Here is the basic recipe, with plenty of flavours to follow to keep you occupied.

PISTACHIO

SPICED FIG

VANILLA

SOYA MILK ICE CREAM

Bring the soya milk to simmering point in a medium saucepan. Meanwhile, whisk the egg yolks and sugar together in a bowl. Pour on the hot milk and mix well. Return the mixture to the pan and cook over a low heat, whisking occasionally, until the custard begins to thicken. Remove from the heat and blitz with a hand blender until it is completely smooth. Add the soya cream and whisk together well. Allow to cool, then chill thoroughly, preferably overnight.

Churn in an ice-cream maker until frozen. The ice cream will keep in the freezer for up to 2 weeks.

SERVES 6–8

250ml (1 cup) soya milk, such as Bonsoy

5 egg yolks

125g (½ cup) caster sugar

250ml (1 cup) unsweetened soya cream, such as Alpro Soya Dream

flavouring (see below)

Variations

Vanilla: add 1 tablespoon of vanilla extract and the seeds from 1 vanilla pod to the soya milk before heating.

Prune and Cognac: add 2 tablespoons of finely chopped prunes and 3 tablespoons Cognac to the soya milk before heating.

Elderflower: add 5 tablespoons of elderflower cordial along with the soya cream.

White Chocolate and Raspberry: add 100g (4 ounces) chopped kosher white chocolate to the hot custard and whisk until melted before adding the soya cream. After churning the ice cream, loosely stir in 2 tablespoons of Raspberry Coulis (see page 171) to create a ripple effect. Freeze as normal.

Cinnamon: add 1 tablespoon of ground cinnamon to the hot soya milk.

Black Pepper: add 1 tablespoon of finely cracked black pepper to the soya milk before heating.

Amaretto: add 3 tablespoons of Amaretto liqueur to the soya milk before heating.

Basil: add 2 tablespoons of finely sliced basil to the final mixture as it cools, before chilling.

Spiced Fig: add 2 tablespoons of Spiced Fig Compote (see page 175) to the hot custard before adding the soya cream.

Lavender: add 3 tablespoons of Lavender Syrup (see page 171) to the soya milk before heating and reduce the amount of caster sugar to 100g (scant ½ cup).

Chocolate: add 100g (4 ounces) of chopped kosher dark chocolate to the hot custard and whisk until melted before adding the soya cream.

DATE AND PISTACHIO FILO PARCELS WITH VANILLA ICE CREAM AND ORANGE AND POMEGRANATE SAUCE

These filo parcels take their inspiration from the little nut- and date-filled pastries of the Middle East, which are served with coffee or mint tea. In this version, the pastry is much flakier, with a moister and slightly chewy filling. It is very moreish and, surprisingly, not too sweet.

For the filling, put the dates, ground pistachios and margarine in a bowl and mix to a rough paste. Stir in the honey and rosewater and set aside.

To make the parcels, brush 2 sheets of filo pastry with melted margarine on both sides and lay them on top of each other. Spoon a heaped tablespoon of the filling in the middle and fold the 4 corners into the centre. Then tuck in the remaining 4 corners produced by the first fold to achieve a rough circular shape. Repeat with the remaining filling and filo to make 6 parcels in total.

Place the parcels on a baking sheet lined with baking parchment and bake in an oven preheated to 200°C/400°F/Gas Mark 6 for 12–15 minutes, until crisp and lightly browned. Serve warm, topped with a ball of vanilla ice cream and drizzled with the pomegranate sauce.

SERVES 6

12 squares of filo pastry, about 15 x 15cm (6 x 6 inches)

125g (½ cup) Tomor margarine, melted

Vanilla Ice Cream (see page 146)

Orange and Pomegranate Sauce (see page 170)

FOR THE FILLING:

200g (7 ounces) dates, finely chopped

200g (7 ounces) ground pistachio nuts

200g (7 ounces) Tomor margarine, softened

200ml (7 ounces) honey

1 tablespoon rosewater

BREADS
&BAKING

RYE AND RED ONION BREAD

This traditional central European bread is flavoured with caraway seeds (kummel) and goes well with pickled herring and smoked salmon.

Put the soya milk and water in a small saucepan and heat until lukewarm. Remove from the heat and whisk in the honey, dried yeast and 100g ($^2/_3$ cup) of the white flour. Leave to stand for 15 minutes.

Meanwhile, heat the groundnut oil in a small saucepan, add the onion and fry gently for 7–8 minutes, until softened but not coloured. Leave to cool for 5 minutes, then add to the liquid mixture and stir well.

In a large mixing bowl, combine the rest of the white flour with the rye flour, salt and caraway seeds and make a well in the centre. Pour in the liquid batter and mix to a soft dough. Turn out and knead on a lightly floured surface for about 10 minutes, until smooth. Return the dough to the mixing bowl, cover with a damp tea towel and leave for 2 hours or until doubled in size.

Knock back the dough to its original size and place in a 1kg (2$^1/_4$ -pound) non-stick loaf tin. Cover with a damp tea towel and leave for about 1$^1/_2$ hours, until doubled in size. Place in an oven preheated to 180°C/350°F/Gas Mark 4 and bake for 40–45 minutes, until the loaf is lightly browned and the base sounds hollow when tapped underneath. Turn out on to a wire rack and leave to cool. This bread is best eaten a day after baking.

MAKES 1 LARGE LOAF

200ml (scant 1 cup) soya milk

150ml ($^2/_3$ cup) water

1 tablespoon honey

1 teaspoon dried yeast

375g (2$^1/_2$ cups) strong white flour

2 tablespoons groundnut oil

1 red onion, finely chopped

225g (1$^1/_2$ cups) rye flour

1 teaspoon fine salt

1 tablespoon caraway seeds

CHALLAH ROLLS WITH POPPY SEEDS

MAKES 12

250ml (1 cup) lukewarm water

2 tablespoons dried yeast

a large pinch of saffron strands

2 tablespoons caster sugar

4 eggs

2 tablespoons honey

1 tablespoon salt

2 tablespoons groundnut oil

650g (4⅓ cups) strong white flour

4 tablespoons poppy seeds

Challah is the Jewish plaited Sabbath bread, where a blessing is made over 2 loaves. Here we have individual rolls, which can be enjoyed any time of the week.

Put the warm water in a bowl, add the dried yeast, saffron and caster sugar and leave to stand for 10 minutes. Separate 2 of the eggs and set the yolks aside. Lightly beat the whites with the remaining 2 eggs. Add to the yeast mixture with the honey, salt and oil and whisk well.

Put the flour in a mixing bowl and make a well in the centre. Pour in the liquid and gradually mix in the flour to make a soft dough. Turn out on to a lightly floured surface and knead for 10 minutes, until smooth and elastic. Lightly grease the dough with a little oil and return it to the bowl. Cover with cling film and leave in a warm place for 2 hours or until doubled in size.

Knock the dough back to its original size, cut it into 12 pieces and shape them into rolls. Place on a greased baking sheet, cover with a damp tea towel and leave to prove for 1 hour, until they have doubled in size. Lightly beat the remaining egg yolks and use to brush the tops of the rolls. Sprinkle with the poppy seeds and bake in an oven preheated to 180°C/350°F/Gas Mark 4 for 20 minutes, until golden brown. Best eaten within one day.

SESAME BAGELS

The European bracelet bread, symbolising the eternal cycle of life, bagels are now seen as the national bread of New York, where they are served for breakfast or lunch with more fillings than you can shake a street vendor's stick at!

Put the warm water in a bowl, whisk in the yeast with a pinch of sugar and leave to stand for 10 minutes. Add the egg yolks, oil, salt and 2 tablespoons of caster sugar and whisk well.

Put the flour in a mixing bowl, make a well in the centre and pour in the liquid. Gradually mix together to form a soft dough. Turn out on to a lightly floured surface and knead for 10 minutes, until smooth and elastic. Lightly grease the dough with oil and return it to the bowl. Cover with cling film and leave in a warm place for 1½ hours or until doubled in size.

Knock the dough back to its original size and cut it into 12 pieces. Roll each into a doughnut shape and make a hole in the middle with your finger. Place the bagels on a greased baking tray, cover with a damp tea towel and leave to prove for 1 hour or until doubled in size.

Poach the bagels in a large pan of simmering water for 2 minutes at most, turning them over as they float to the surface. Place immediately on a tea towel and gently pat dry, then put them back on the greased baking tray. Lightly beat the egg whites and use to brush the bagels. Sprinkle them with the sesame seeds and bake in an oven preheated to 190°C/375°F/Gas Mark 5 for 15 minutes, until golden brown. These are best eaten fresh or within a few hours.

MAKES 12

150ml (2/3 cup) lukewarm water

1 teaspoon dried yeast

2 tablespoons caster sugar, plus an extra pinch

2 eggs, separated

4 teaspoons groundnut oil

1 teaspoon salt

550g (3 2/3 cups) strong white flour

4 tablespoons sesame seeds

HONEY CAKE

Honey cake is the traditional Ashkenazi cake for Rosh Hashanah, the Jewish New Year, carrying hopes for sweetness and fulfilment in the coming year.

In a large mixing bowl, whisk the eggs and sugar together until pale and fluffy. Then add the oil, honey and orange zest and mix well. Gradually mix in the ground spices and flour until the batter is smooth. Separately mix the bicarbonate of soda with the orange juice and pour it into the mixture, which will now be quite runny. Pour into a 25 x 20 x 5cm (10 x 8 x 2 inch) baking tin lined with baking parchment and place in an oven preheated to 180°C/350°F/Gas Mark 4. Bake for 45–55 minutes, until firm but springy. Leave to cool in the tin, then carefully wrap in cling film and foil and store in a cupboard for 2–3 days, so the cake becomes moist. Serve with coffee, tea or Kiddush wine. This cake improves with age, becoming wonderfully rich and moist after 4 days of so.

2 eggs

75g ($\frac{1}{3}$ cup) caster sugar

100ml (scant $\frac{1}{2}$ cup) groundnut oil

200ml (scant 1 cup) honey

juice and grated zest of 1 orange

1 teaspoon ground mixed spice

1 teaspoon ground cinnamon

$\frac{1}{2}$ teaspoon ground ginger

175g (1$\frac{1}{6}$ cups) plain flour

1 teaspoon bicarbonate of soda

SHORTCRUST PASTRY

This is a good, basic shortcrust that can be used for almost any kind of tart or pie.

Put the flour in a mixing bowl, add the margarine and rub them together between your fingers and thumbs until the mixture resembles rough breadcrumbs. Add the salt and pepper. Whisk the egg and milk together, then add to the flour mixture and mix to a smooth dough. Wrap in cling film and refrigerate for 30 minutes before using.

FOR 1 TART CASE

250g (1$\frac{2}{3}$ cups) plain flour

150g ($\frac{2}{3}$ cup) Tomor margarine, cut into 1cm ($\frac{1}{2}$-inch) dice

a pinch each of salt and pepper

1 egg

1 tablespoon soya milk

ALMOND BRANDY SNAPS

MAKES 16–20

100g (²/₃ cup) plain flour

100g (scant ½ cup) Tomor margarine, melted

100ml (scant ½ cup) golden syrup

100g (scant ½ cup) caster sugar

1 teaspoon ground ginger

2 tablespoons nibbed almonds

These golden, crisp, wafer-thin biscuits accompany the Vanilla and Peach Crème Brûlée on page 126 but can also be served as petits fours.

Put all the ingredients in a small bowl and mix to a smooth paste. (The mixture will keep in the fridge for up to 2 weeks.) Chill for 2–3 hours, until firm. Then break off walnut-sized pieces, roll them into small balls and place on a large baking sheet lined with baking parchment, leaving at least 5cm (2-inches) between them. Press each one down with your thumb. Bake in an oven preheated to 190°C/375°F/Gas Mark 5 for 6–7 minutes, until golden brown; they will still be very soft. Remove the tray from the oven and allow to rest for 1 minute only. Then, with a palette knife, carefully lift up each brandy snap and drape it over a greased rolling pin. Leave for about 2–3 minutes, until set hard, then remove. The brandy snaps will keep in an airtight container for up to 3 days.

SWEET PASTRY

FOR TWO TART CASES

500g (3¹/₃ cups) plain flour

125g (½ cup) caster sugar

250g (1 cup) Tomor margarine, cut into 1cm (½-inch) dice

1 egg and 1 egg yolk, beaten

seeds from 1 vanilla pod (optional)

This sweet pastry is used for the Frangipane and Elderberry Tart on page 127 but would work well with any sweet tart.

Combine the flour and sugar in a mixing bowl, then add the margarine. Rub them together between your fingers and thumbs until the mixture resembles rough breadcrumbs. Add the beaten egg and the vanilla seeds, if using, and mix to form a smooth dough. Cover in cling film and refrigerate for 30 minutes before using.

ROSEWATER MACAROONS

These subtle, fragrant biscuits are good with peppermint tea and other herbal infusions. They also go well with Watermelon Granita (see page 142).

Put all the dry ingredients in a small bowl and mix well, then add the egg white and rosewater. Mix to a smooth paste and refrigerate for 30 minutes. Then divide the mixture into 10 walnut-sized pieces and roll each one carefully between the palms of your hands into a small ball. Gently press down to form a disc about 5mm (¼-inch) thick and place on a greased baking sheet. Bake in an oven preheated to 160°C/325°F/Gas Mark 3 for 12–15 minutes, until pale golden. Remove from the oven and place on a wire rack to cool. Store in an airtight container for 2 days at most.

MAKES 10

125g (1 heaped cup) ground almonds

75g (⅓ cup) caster sugar

2 teaspoons cornflour

½ teaspoon baking powder

1 egg white

1 tablespoon rosewater

LAVENDER SHORTBREAD

These lovely biscuits are served with the Summer Berry Gruetze on page 138 but are also delicious on their own.

Beat the margarine and sugar together in a bowl until pale and creamy. Add the flour, cornmeal and lavender and mix to a smooth paste, then refrigerate for half an hour. On a floured surface, gently roll out the dough to 5–6mm (¼-inch) thick. Cut out whatever shapes you like with a pastry cutter, or simply cut it into 1.5 x 5cm (½ x 2 inch) oblongs with a knife. Prick with a fork, sprinkle with caster sugar and place on a baking sheet lined with baking parchment. Place in an oven preheated to 160°C/325°C/Gas Mark 3 and bake for 12–15 minutes, until pale golden. Transfer to a wire rack to cool.

MAKES 6–12

100g (scant ½ cup) Tomor margarine, softened

50g (¼ cup) caster sugar, plus extra for sprinkling

100g (⅔ cup) plain flour

50g (½ cup) cornmeal or fine polenta

1 tablespoon dried lavender buds

SAUCES
PICKLES
&
CHUTNEYS

RED WINE GRAVY

This wonderful rich sauce accompanies the rack of lamb on page 84 and also, enhanced with cassis, the roast duck breasts on page 93. It would also go well with any roast dinner.

Heat the margarine in a saucepan, add the shallots and fry gently for 5–6 minutes without colouring. Then increase the heat to high, add the red wine and simmer until reduced to 100ml (scant ½ cup). Pour in the hot broth and simmer until reduced by half; the sauce should be thick enough to coat the back of a spoon lightly. Season with salt and pepper if necessary.

SERVES 4

50g (3 tablespoons) Tomor margarine

2 shallots, finely chopped

500ml (2 cups) red wine

500ml (2 cups) hot Chicken Broth (see page 24)

sea salt and black pepper

MILANESE SAUCE

Milanese sauce is a classic, traditionally served with breaded cutlets or escalopes. It also makes a great pasta sauce, especially with spaghetti or linguine.

Heat the olive oil in a saucepan, add the mushrooms and smoked beef and fry over a high heat for 2 minutes, until lightly browned. Add the tomato purée and fry for 1 minute, then pour in the chicken broth and stir to make a smooth sauce. Add the chopped tomatoes, bring to the boil and simmer for 10 minutes, stirring occasionally. Add the cooked tongue and truffle and season to taste with salt and pepper.

SERVES 4

2 tablespoons olive oil

50g (2 ounces) mushrooms, cut into thin strips

50g (2 ounces) smoked beef

1 tablespoon tomato purée

200ml (scant 1 cup) Chicken Broth (see page 24)

220g (1 cup) canned chopped tomatoes

50g (2 ounces) cooked tongue, cut into thin strips

20g (¾ ounce) black truffle (a canned one is fine), cut into thin strips

sea salt and black pepper

COARSEGRAIN MUSTARD SAUCE

SERVES 4

50g (3 tablespoons) Tomor margarine

2 shallots, finely chopped

2 tablespoons coarsegrain mustard

350ml (1½ cups) hot Vegetable Stock (see page 25)

125ml (½ cup) unsweetened soya cream

1 tablespoon lemon juice

sea salt and black pepper

This is a lovely, sharp-tasting sauce, which goes very well with steamed vegetables or poached fish – for example, the smoked haddock on page 72.

Heat the margarine in a saucepan, add the shallots and fry gently for 5–6 minutes without colouring. Stir in the mustard and raise the heat. Pour in the hot vegetable stock and simmer for 5 minutes. Finally add the soya cream and lemon juice. Bring almost to the boil, whisking constantly, then remove from the heat and season to taste.

CIDER SAUCE

SERVES 4

50g (3 tablespoons) Tomor margarine

1 Granny Smith apple, peeled, cored and cut into 5mm (¼-inch) dice

300ml (1¼ cups) dry cider

500ml (2 cups) hot Fish Stock (see page 25)

125ml (½ cup) unsweetened soya cream

1 tablespoon lemon juice

sea salt and ground white pepper

This mild velouté sauce marries perfectly with round or flat white fish, such as Grey Mullet with Swiss Chard (see page 67).

Heat the margarine in a saucepan, add the diced apple and fry over a high heat for 1–2 minutes, until lightly browned. Add the cider and simmer until reduced to 100ml (scant ¼ cup). Pour in the hot fish stock and simmer until reduced by half. Finally add the soya cream and lemon juice and bring almost to the boil, whisking constantly. Remove from the heat and season to taste.

PAPRIKA SAUCE

SAUCE ANGLAISE

164

PESTO

MILANESE SAUCE

RED WINE FISH SAUCE

Serve this rich sauce with robust fish dishes, such as Sea Bass with Aubergine Caviar (see page 64).

Heat the margarine in a saucepan, add the shallots and fry gently for 5–6 minutes without colouring. Then increase the heat to high, add the red wine and port or Adamo and simmer until reduced to 100ml (scant ½ cup). Pour in the hot fish stock and simmer until reduced by half; the sauce should be thick enough to coat the back of a spoon lightly. Season to taste with salt and pepper.

SERVES 4

50g (3 tablespoons) Tomor margarine

2 shallots, finely chopped

350ml (1½ cups) red wine

150ml (⅔ cup) kosher port or Adamo

500ml (2 cups) Fish Stock (see page 25)

sea salt and black pepper

HONEY AND MUSTARD DRESSING

This attractive dressing is good with fish and meat, as well as simple leaf salads.

Simply whisk all the ingredients together in a bowl until smooth. Store in a small plastic container or a squeezy bottle.

SERVES 4

1 tablespoon coarsegrain mustard

1 tablespoon honey

1 teaspoon Dijon mustard

2 tablespoons cider vinegar

6 tablespoons groundnut oil

1 teaspoon fine sea salt

½ teaspoon ground white pepper

LEMON DRESSING

The classic Mediterranean dressing for all types of salad, this can also be used as a light accompanying sauce for baked or roasted fish.

SERVES 4
1 tablespoon lemon juice
1 teaspoon finely grated lemon zest
4 tablespoons extra virgin olive oil
1/2 teaspoon English mustard
1 teaspoon fine sea salt
1/2 teaspoon ground white pepper

Whisk all the ingredients together in a bowl until smooth. Store in a small plastic container or a squeezy bottle.

PAPRIKA SAUCE

In Central Europe red peppers – both the fresh vegetable and the ground spice – are referred to as paprika. This mild, smoky sauce can be served with many dishes. It goes well with grilled meats, steamed or roasted fish and all types of pasta, including ravioli, tortellini and Potato and Thyme Gnocchi (see page 106).

Heat the olive oil in a small saucepan, add the shallots and fry gently for 5–6 minutes without colouring. Increase the heat to high and add the smoked paprika and tomato purée, Fry for 1 minute, stirring all the time, then add the roasted peppers and vegetable stock and bring to the boil. Reduce the heat and simmer for 5 minutes. Remove from the heat and blitz with a hand blender until very smooth. Pass through a fine sieve and season to taste.

SERVES 4

1 tablespoon olive oil

2 shallots, finely chopped

1 teaspoon smoked paprika

1 teaspoon tomato purée

200g (7 ounces) roasted red peppers, finely chopped (from a jar is fine)

400ml (1 2/3 cups) Vegetable Stock (see page 25)

sea salt and black pepper

SWEET BALSAMIC SAUCE

This sweet and sour dessert sauce accompanies the Strawberry and Shortbread Tart on page 135. You could also serve it drizzled over summer strawberries, topped with a few grinds of fresh black pepper.

Put the vinegar in a small saucepan and simmer gently over a medium heat for 4–5 minutes, to reduce its acidity. Then add the honey, bring to the boil and simmer for 2 minutes. Remove from the heat and leave to cool.

SERVES 4

4 tablespoons balsamic vinegar

2 tablespoons honey

SAUCE ANGLAISE

SERVES 4

250ml (1 cup) soya milk,
  such as Bonsoy

250ml (1 cup) unsweetened
  soya cream

1 tablespoon natural vanilla
  extract

seeds from 1 vanilla pod

4 egg yolks

125g (½ cup) caster sugar

Sauce anglaise is the traditional English egg custard, served as a warm or chilled sauce or as the basis for many hot and cold desserts. Usually the custard is stirred with a wooden spoon until it has thickened and then strained to get rid of little lumps. As this recipe is made with soya cream and soya milk, however, it's not necessary. You can whisk the sauce continually until it begins to thicken, hence avoiding those lumps, and it doesn't become frothy, as a dairy-based custard would.

Bring the soya milk, cream and vanilla extract and seeds to simmering point in a small saucepan, then set aside. Meanwhile, whisk the egg yolks and caster sugar together until pale and fluffy. Pour on the hot liquid, whisking continuously, then return the sauce to the cleaned pan and cook gently, whisking all the time, until it begins to thicken. Remove from the heat and allow to cool slightly, whisking occasionally. Serve warm or leave to cool completely and store in the fridge for up to for 3 days.

Variation: Pistachio Anglaise
Follow the recipe above but replace the vanilla extract and seeds with 1 tablespoon of pistachio paste. If you cannot obtain pistachio paste, use 2 tablespoons of pistachio nuts and grind them finely in a food processor, then add 1 teaspoon of vegetable oil and process again.

CHOCOLATE SAUCE

This decadent sauce is the perfect accompaniment to all chocolate desserts and puddings. It also goes well with desserts based on almonds, hazelnuts and pistachios and is a great sauce to serve with ice cream.

Put the water, sugar and Cointreau, if using, in a small saucepan and bring to the boil, stirring to dissolve the sugar. Simmer for 2 minutes, then remove from the heat and whisk in the chopped chocolate until completely melted. Serve warm, or leave to cool and store in an airtight container for up to 1 week.

SERVES 4–6

150ml (²/₃ cup) water

100g (scant ½ cup) caster sugar

25ml (5 teaspoons) Cointreau (optional)

100g (4 ounces) kosher dark chocolate, finely chopped

ORANGE & POMEGRANATE SAUCE

A tangy citrus syrup that can be served with desserts and some savoury dishes, such as Pâté de Foie Gras (see page 41).

Put all the ingredients in a small saucepan and bring to the boil, stirring to dissolve the sugar. Simmer for about 10–15 minutes, until the sauce is thick enough to coat the back of a spoon, then leave to cool. Store, covered, in a cool place.

MAKES 300ML (1¼ CUPS)

250ml (1 cup) orange juice

175g (³/₄ cup) caster sugar

1 teaspoon pomegranate syrup

APPLE COULIS

SERVES 4

3 Granny Smith apples

200ml (scant 1 cup) water

50g (¼ cup) caster sugar

juice of 1 lemon

This fruit sauce accompanies Lockshen Pudding (see page 130) and can also be served with creams and mousses.

Cut the apples into 1cm (½-inch) dice, skin, core and all, and place in a saucepan with the water, sugar and lemon. Cook over a low heat for about 10 minutes, until the mixture becomes a purée. Blend in a food processor for 2 minutes, until almost liquid, then pass through a very fine sieve. Leave to cool. The coulis will keep in the fridge for up to 1 week.

RASPBERRY COULIS

SERVES 4

300g (1⅓ cups) fresh raspberries

100g (scant ½ cup) caster sugar

A marvellous, fresh-tasting dessert sauce, unobtrusive and very versatile.

Place the raspberries in a bowl, sprinkle with the sugar and leave to stand for 10 minutes to allow the sugar to draw the juices from the fruit. Then place in a food processor and blend to a smooth purée. Pass the mixture through a fine sieve. Store in a plastic container or a squeezy bottle in the fridge for up to 3 days.

LAVENDER SYRUP

MAKES 300ML (1¼ CUPS)

200ml (scant 1 cup) water

125g (½ cup) caster sugar

1 tablespoon dried lavender buds

3 tablespoons blue Curaçao

25ml (5 teaspoons) grenadine syrup

I use this versatile syrup to flavour ice creams and cocktails. You could also add it to fruit salads and compotes.

Combine all the ingredients in a small saucepan, bring to the boil and simmer for 3 minutes. Remove from the heat and leave to cool, then strain into a small, sterilised bottle or jar. The syrup will keep for up to 1 month.

NEW GREEN CUCUMBERS

The traditional Jewish accompaniment to hot salt beef, these also go well with cold sliced meats and even chopped liver. Acetic acid is available from kosher shops.

Cut the cucumbers in half lengthways and then cut them into pieces to fit your chosen plastic container (about 3 litres/12 cups in volume). Put them in the container, then stir the rest of the ingredients together and pour them over the cucumbers. Seal the container and refrigerate for 3 days. To serve, slice the cucumbers into bite-sized pieces. They will keep for about a week in the fridge.

SERVES 6-8

3 large cucumbers

1.5 litres (6 cups) water

100g (4 ounces) fine sea salt

100g (scant ½ cup) caster sugar

2 tablespoons acetic acid

6 garlic cloves, peeled and halved

1 red chilli, deseeded and finely sliced

4 bay leaves

20 coriander seeds

CHRANE

This relish is the traditional sauce to accompany Hot Salt Beef and Chips (see page 79).

Mix all the ingredients together in a bowl. It will keep in the fridge for up to a week.

SERVES 4-6

250g (9 ounces) cooked beetroot, finely grated

3 tablespoons finely grated horseradish

1 Granny Smith apple, cored and coarsely grated

1 tablespoon cider vinegar

1 teaspoon fine sea salt

½ teaspoon ground white pepper

PICCALILLI

APPLE AND RAISIN CHUTNEY

SLICED FIG COMPOTE

NEW GREEN CUCUMBERS

PESTO

The famous pasta sauce of Genoa, pesto is traditionally made with a little Pecorino cheese. This dairy-free version tastes just as good and is arguably healthier to boot!

Blitz the basil, pine nuts, garlic and lemon to a smooth paste in a food processor, then drizzle the olive oil in, little by little. Season to taste with salt and pepper. The pesto will keep in the fridge for up to a week.

leaves from 2 bunches of basil

4 tablespoons pine nuts, lightly toasted

2 garlic cloves, peeled

juice of 1/2 lemon

250ml (1 cup) extra virgin oil

sea salt and black pepper

BEETROOT HARISSA

Harissa is a fiery chilli paste from North Africa, toned down here with mild cooked beetroot. Traditionally it is served with soups and tagines, such as Lamb and Apricot Tagine (see page 86).

Simply mix all the ingredients together in a bowl until fully combined. Store in the fridge for up to 1 week.

250g (9 ounces) cooked beetroot, finely grated

2 tablespoons harissa paste

juice of 1/2 lemon

1/2 teaspoon sea salt

CHUTNEYS

Below is a selection of classic sweet and sour chutneys and pickles, all of which will complement cold meats, pâtés and chopped liver.

APPLE AND RAISIN CHUTNEY

MAKES ABOUT 500g
(1 pound 2 ounces)

1 tablespoon groundnut oil

1 onion, cut into 1cm (1/2-inch) dice

1 tablespoon white mustard seeds

3 tablespoons cider vinegar

2 tablespoons raisins

2 tablespoons honey

3 Granny Smith apples, peeled,
   cored and cut into 1cm
   (1/2-inch) dice

Heat the oil in a saucepan, add the onion and mustard seeds and fry over a medium heat for 2 minutes without colouring. Add the vinegar and raisins and cook for 2 minutes. Finally add the honey and apples and cook for about 10 minutes, stirring occasionally until the apple softens. Remove from the heat and leave to cool. The chutney will keep in an airtight container in the fridge for up to 1 week.

SPICED FIG COMPOTE

MAKES ABOUT 500g
(1 pound 2 ounces)

250g (9 ounces) dried figs, finely
   chopped

200ml (scant 1 cup) honey

juice and grated zest of 1 lemon

500ml (2 cups) water

2 tablespoons ground cinnamon

1 tablespoon ground mixed spice

1 tablespoon vanilla extract

Put all the ingredients in a saucepan and bring to the boil over a medium heat. Simmer for 25–30 minutes or until almost all the liquid has been absorbed and the mixture has become a thick, syrupy paste. Leave to cool. It will keep in an airtight container in the fridge for up to 2 weeks.

PICCALILLI

In a large shallow tray, mix the cauliflower, cucumbers and onions with the salt. Refrigerate overnight. Then wash the vegetables in cold water and pat dry.

Bring the cider vinegar, chillies, garlic and vegetable stock to the boil in a large saucepan and simmer until reduced by half. Add the mustard and honey and bring back to the boil. Meanwhile, mix the cornflour and ground spices with the water to make a thin paste. Whisk it into the boiling liquid until it starts to thicken, then add the vegetables.

Mix well and cook for 2 minutes, then remove from the heat and leave to cool. It will keep in an airtight container in the fridge for up to 2 weeks.

MAKES ABOUT 1kg (2¼ pounds)

1 cauliflower, cut into 1cm (½-inch) dice

3 cucumbers, peeled, deseeded and cut into 1cm (½-inch) dice

2 onions, cut into 1cm (½-inch) dice

200g (7 ounces) fine sea salt

500ml (2 cups) cider vinegar

4 red chillies, deseeded and finely sliced

4 garlic cloves, finely sliced

250ml (1 cup) Vegetable Stock (see page 25)

200g (scant 1 cup) coarsegrain mustard

200ml (scant 1 cup) honey

2 tablespoons cornflour

1 tablespoon ground turmeric

1 tablespoon ground ginger

1 teaspoon ground fennel seeds

1 tablespoon water

APRICOT AND LAVENDER COMPOTE

Put all the ingredients in a small saucepan and bring to the boil. Remove from the heat and leave to cool. The compote will keep in an airtight container in the fridge for up to 1 week.

MAKES ABOUT 350g (12 ounces)

250g (9 ounces) canned apricots, drained and cut into 5mm (¼-inch) dice

125ml (½ cup) honey

1 tablespoon dried lavender buds

TOMATO AND SHALLOT CHUTNEY

MAKES ABOUT 500g (1 pound 2 ounces)

2 tablespoons olive oil

250g (9 ounces) shallots, cut into 1cm (1/2-inch) dice

2 tablespoons white mustard seeds

2 tablespoons soft brown sugar

2 tablespoons cider vinegar

2 bay leaves

400g (1²/₃ cups) canned chopped tomatoes

sea salt and black pepper

Heat the olive oil in a saucepan, add the shallots and mustard seeds and fry over a medium heat for 2 minutes without colouring. Then add the sugar and cook for 1 minute. Add the cider vinegar and bay leaves and cook for another minute. Finally add the chopped tomatoes and simmer for 10 minutes, stirring occasionally. Season to taste. Remove from the heat and leave to cool. The chutney will keep in an airtight container in the fridge for up to 1 week.

DAMSON AND RED ONION CHUTNEY

MAKES ABOUT 500g (1 pound 2 ounces)

2 tablespoons groundnut oil

2 red onions, cut into 1cm (1/2-inch) dice

2 tablespoons poppy seeds

2 tablespoons cider vinegar

2 tablespoons honey

500g (1 pound 2 ounces) damsons (or plums), pitted and cut into 1cm (1/2-inch) dice

Heat the groundnut oil in a saucepan, add the red onions and poppy seeds and fry for 2 minutes without colouring. Add the cider vinegar and cook for a further minute. Then add the honey and diced damsons and simmer for 10 minutes. Remove from the heat and leave to cool. It will keep in an airtight container in the fridge for up to 1 week.

COCKTAILS

BEVIS MARKS COCKTAILS

These cocktails were inspired by the sacred fruits of the Jewish year and its various festivals (see pages 17–18). There is something here to suit all tastes: the sweet and sour daiquiri, a spiced opera, a creamy martini, along with a more classical martini scented with lavender, plus refreshing long drinks such as a tropical-flavoured sling, a Central European-inspired Collins, and an apple shmooze that mirrors the flavours of the traditional Jewish lockshen pudding – something to chat, gossip, lay back and relax with!

ALL COCKTAILS SERVE 1.

BM COLLINS

25ml cherry brandy
25ml slivovitz (plum brandy)
25ml elderflower cordial
15ml lemon juice
tonic water

Place some ice cubes in a cocktail shaker and pour in the cherry brandy, slivovitz, elderflower and lemon juice. Shake well and strain into a hi-ball or Collins glass. Top up with tonic water.

BM SLING

50ml gin
25ml Midori (melon liqueur)
25ml honey
50ml pineapple juice
ginger ale

Place some ice cubes in a cocktail shaker, pour in the gin, Midori, honey and pineapple juice, then shake well. Strain into a sling glass, add a couple of ice cubes and top up with ginger ale.

CITY TRADER

50ml vodka
25ml Midori (melon liqueur)
25ml red grape juice

Place some ice cubes in a cocktail shaker and pour in all the ingredients. Shake well and leave to rest for 1 minute. Shake again, then strain into a chilled martini glass.

BM COLLINS

BM SLING

BM OPERA

LAVENDER MARTINI

GHERKIN MARTINI

BM DAQUIRI

BEVIS MARKS COCKTAILS

BM DAIQUIRI

65ml white rum
15ml Midori (melon liqueur)
15ml pomegranate syrup
15ml lime juice

Pour all the ingredients into a cocktail shaker, add some ice and shake well. Leave to rest for 1 minute, then shake again. Strain into a chilled martini glass.

BM OPERA

50ml Kiddush (Sabbath) wine
25ml gin
25ml Cointreau
10ml Goldstrike (cinnamon schnapps)
4 drops of angostura bitters

Place some ice cubes in a cocktail shaker, pour in all the ingredients and shake well for about 20 seconds. Strain into a martini glass.

PASSOVER

50ml vodka
the pulp of 2 passionfruit
150ml grapefruit juice

Place some ice cubes into a cocktail shaker and pour in all the ingredients. Shake well for about 20 seconds, then strain through a fine sieve into a Collins glass and top up with fresh ice.

BM MARTINI

35ml vodka
35ml crème de cacao
25ml cherry brandy
15ml Amaretto
35ml soya cream
a pinch of grated nutmeg

Place some ice cubes in a cocktail shaker, pour in all the ingredients except the nutmeg and shake well for about 20 seconds. Strain into a martini glass and garnish with the nutmeg.

LAVENDER MARTINI

65ml vodka
15ml Martini Bianco
10ml Lavender Syrup (see page 171)
15ml Parfait Amour

Pour all the ingredients into a cocktail shaker, top up with ice cubes and shake well. Leave to rest for 1 minute, then shake again. Strain into a chilled martini glass.

GHERKIN MARTINI

65ml vodka
15ml Martini Bianco
15ml Midori (melon liqueur)
cocktail onion and cornichon

Place some ice cubes in a cocktail shaker, pour in the vodka, Martini and Midori and shake well. Leave to rest for 1 minute, then shake again and strain into a chilled martini glass. Garnish with a cocktail onion and a cornichon, skewered with a cocktail stick.

APPLE SHMOOZE

25ml Cognac

25ml limoncello

15ml Goldstrike
(cinnamon schnapps)

15ml lemon juice

100ml apple juice

Pour all the ingredients into a
cocktail shaker, top up with ice
and shake well for about 20
seconds. Then strain into a
hurricane glass or large wine glass
and top up with fresh ice cubes.

OUR SUPPLIERS

Featured below is a list of our restaurant suppliers, with our appreciation for your continued support and service, and with best wishes for a prosperous future.

GILBERTS KOSHER FOODS LTD
Suppliers of fresh & cooked
kosher meat
Mount Avenue, Mount Farm, Bletchley
Milton Keynes, Bucks MK1 1LS
TEL: 01908 646 787
FAX: 01908 646 788

KOSHER DELI
Suppliers of kosher deli products, fresh
& cooked meats
132 Golders Green Road
London NW11 8HB
TEL: 020 8381 4450
FAX: 020 8731 6450

EUROPE KOSHER LTD
Suppliers of French poultry, including
duck, corn-fed chicken and foie gras
26 Woodville Road
London NW11 9TN
TEL: 020 8458 0055
FAX: 020 8458 6633

H.S. LINWOOD & SONS LTD
Suppliers of fresh fish in the heart of
the City of London
6–7 Grand Avenue, Leadenhall Market
London EC3V 1LR
TEL: 020 7929 0554
FAX: 020 7929 2194

PENTA FOODS LTD
Purveyors of fine & oriental foods, dry
stores and provisions
30 Wellington Road, Sandhurst
Berkshire GU47 9AY
TEL: 0845 051 0223
FAX: 0845 051 0224
WEB: www.pentafoods.com

MARIGOLD HEALTH FOOD LTD
Suppliers of organic & wholefood
produce (also wholesalers for Bonsoy
Soya-milk and Alpro Soya Dream)
102 Camley Street
London NW1 OPF
TEL: 020 7388 4515
FAX: 020 7388 4516

PRESCOTT THOMAS LTD
Suppliers of fresh, frozen and
speciality fruit & vegetables
Unit 1 Horner House, New Spitalfields
Market
21 Sherrin Road, Leyton
London E10 5SQ
TEL: 020 8558 9550
FAX: 020 8558 3028
E-MAIL: info@prescott-thomas.com
WEB: www.prescott-thomas.com

KEDEM EUROPE LIMITED
Suppliers of kosher wine from
around the world
10 Timberwharf Road
London N16 6DB
TEL: 020 8802 8889
FAX: 020 8809 2880

WORLD WINE EXCHANGE LTD
Suppliers of worldwide kosher wines
65 Maygrove Road
London NW6 2EH
TEL: 020 7692 2020
FAX: 020 7692 2022
E-MAIL: info@worldwineXchange.com

ABEN WINES LTD
Suppliers of fine kosher wines,
Champagne, liqueurs and spirits
Access Business Centre
Wembley Stadium Industrial Estate
First Way, Wembley, Middlesex HA9
OHB
TEL: 020 8900 9427
FAX: 020 8795 2468
WEB: www.abenwines.co.uk

W & F FISH LTD
Smoked salmon specialists
56–64 Crogsland Road
Chalk Farm
London NW1 8AU
TEL: 020 7485 6603
FAX: 020 7284 3059

J.GRODZINSKI & DAUGHTERS
London family bakers since 1888
9 Northways Parade
Swiss Cottage, London
TEL: 020 7722 4944
WEB: www.grodzinski.co.uk

INDEX